A Charming Place

BATH IN THE LIFE AND NOVELS OF JANE AUSTEN

by
MAGGIE LANE

ILLUSTRATIONS BY BRIDGET SUDWORTH

Millstream Books

To Ripple

in commemoration of
a quarter of a century
of friendship

First published 1988
Amended reprint 1993

Millstream Books
7 Orange Grove
Bath BA1 1LP

This book has been set in 10pt Plantin by
Character Graphics, Taunton

Printed by The Matthews Wright Press, Chard

© Maggie Lane 1988

Illustrations © Bridget Sudworth 1988

ISBN 0 948975 48

Contents

Illustrations

PART ONE

'My Bath Life'

Jane Austen and the city of Bath are closely connected, as a matter of historical fact, and in the modern consciousness. People who appreciate the elegant prose and incisive wit of the one, generally admire the harmony and proportion of the Georgian architecture of the other.

That Bath played a significant part in the life and work of Jane Austen is beyond question. Leisurely visits to the city in the 1790s, and five years residence there from 1801 to 1806, extended her experience and enriched her understanding of contemporary society. This bore fruit in the fiction published between 1811 and 1817. In two of the six novels, Bath provides a specific setting which not only assists the progress of the plot – gives her characters something to *do*, in other words – but helps reveal where they stand on a scale of moral values. Jane Austen could depend upon Bath, its customs and topography, being familiar to her readers. Second only to London, the importance of Bath to the national culture during her lifetime is evident from the fact that none of her novels is without reference to the city, whether the story takes us there or not.

There is a sense in which Jane Austen's own story begins in Bath, since it was there, in April 1764, that her parents married. More intriguing, and less well known, perhaps, is the fact that Bath could be said to owe its magnificent appearance – in so far as that was determined by its foremost architect, John Wood – to an ancestor of Jane Austen. Without the involvement of this man at a crucial moment in the city's history, one of Bath's most recent serious historians, Professor R. S. Neale, has declared that Wood 'could never had laid one stone upon another'.[1]

Who was this man, whose name is not normally accorded the prominence of the three famous 'creators' of Georgian Bath – Wood, Ralph Allen and Beau Nash – and whose connection with Jane Austen is similarly little known? He was James Brydges, First Duke of Chandos, whose second wife, Cassandra Willoughby, gave her unusual Christian name to Jane Austen's mother and sister (and her surname to one of Jane's most charming villains). By pausing to examine the brief but decisive participation of Chandos in the development of Bath, we may at the same time gain an understanding of how the city grew into the place

Jane Austen knew so well, and notice how its history was interwoven with that of her family through the course of the 18th century.

The first quarter of the century had seen the establishment of Bath as a unique resort of health and pleasure for people of fashion and expense. They came from their country estates to take the waters, to see and be seen by their social equals, and to occupy their abundant leisure with a variety of novel amusements available nowhere else. An assembly room and a pump room were built; a bowling green and a terrace walk laid out, on a scrap of empty land close by the river. Yet hitherto no effort had been made, either by the Corporation or by private enterprise, to provide these aristocratic and wealthy visitors with decent accommodation. The mediaeval borough walls remained unbreached, enclosing an area of a mere 24 acres, in the narrow, crooked streets and flimsy, dirty buildings of which these increasingly fastidious people were expected to pay for the pleasure of cramming themselves.

Among the visitors in the spring of 1726 were the Duke of Chandos and his duchess Cassandra, in quest of relief from his 'twitching nerves' and her 'hysterical fits'. They may not have found a cure, but the Duke soon spotted an investment opportunity.

He was not new to speculation by any means. Already a millionaire – an amazing achievement considering the money values of the times – he had accumulated a vast personal fortune during 8 years as Paymaster General to the Forces Abroad during Marlborough's campaigns, and he had been multiplying it ever since through intricate and probably questionable international financial dealings. He was unusual in being an aristocrat whose wealth did not chiefly derive from land ownership (though he did possess a mansion, Canons, in Hertfordshire, where his conspicuous consumption gained him the soubriquet 'Princely Chandos').

It was his invariable habit to cloak his dealings in secrecy, and he was especially anxious to conceal his identity in Bath, where the Freemen and Corporation, still parochial in outlook, were likely to be frightened away from doing business with a great Duke. In negotiating to purchase from them a piece of land, to clear the complex lifehold leases and demolish the existing buildings, he therefore acted through a local agent. The Duke next looked around for 'a mason on the spot, who is master of his business, and would also undertake the stonework'. At this time John Wood was 22 years old, and working on nothing more creative than the project to make the river Avon navigable from

Bristol to Bath, which he was paid 1½d per mile to oversee, with 3d per mile for constructing the locks. But he was a man of vision with a talent for self-promotion, and Chandos signed a contract with him on 23 January 1727.[2]

Though in the erection of Chandos Buildings, just within the city walls facing west across open countryside, Wood was allowed little freedom of design, this employment of Wood by Chandos had two far-reaching effects: it infected others with the entrepreneurial spirit, from which the development of Bath slowly gathered momentum; and it led to other commissions for Wood, who was soon sufficiently credit-worthy to begin building speculatively on his own account. Queen Square, North and South Parades, and the King's Circus were the result; pieces of town planning on a scale unimagined before. Extending the city beyond its borough walls, they afforded spaces for promenading, fully integrated with noble terraces of houses in the grand Palladian style. Though by no means all of Wood's grandiose scheme for the creation of a new, pseudo-Roman Bath was realized, his great achievements certainly began, and set the style for, the complete transformation of the city.

The Duke of Chandos had expended £14,426 on buying the land, building and equipping his houses in Bath; they were let at a total rent of £754 10s per annum, which represented a return of just over 5 per cent. Presumably Chandos was dissatisfied with this rate, or disliked the trouble the whole project had cost him, since he dabbled no more in Bath property. The developers of Bath thereafter were all local men, but it was a connection of Jane Austen's family who had shown them that there were profits to be made from building, and who had given the visionary John Wood his first break.

Long before Chandos's fleeting intrusion into the Bath scene, his sister, Mary Brydges, had married Theophilus Leigh of Adlestrop in Gloucestershire, borne him twelve children, and died at the age of 37. One of her sons was Dr Theophilus Leigh, Master of Balliol College, Oxford, for more than half a century. Another was the Reverend Thomas Leigh, who in 1760 or thereabouts retired as Rector of Harpsden in Oxfordshire and settled with his wife and two unmarried daughters, Jane and Cassandra, in Bath. Miss Cassandra Leigh, on a visit to her uncle Theophilus, met 'the handsome proctor' (as he was known) of St John's College, the Reverend George Austen. She was witty and shrewd, he scholarly and serene; they complemented one another intellectually and temperamentally. In all probability he visited her at Bath to continue the courtship; certainly it was there that they were married, in St Swithin's, the parish church of Walcot, in 1764.

Bath must have had happy associations for Mrs Austen, who knew it in its heyday, when it was smaller, more exclusive and more fashionable than it was a generation afterwards, yet more spacious, civilized and beautiful than it had been a generation before. Her consequent affection for Bath was to have repercussions for her daughter Jane – and hence for English literature.

On their marriage the Austens settled at Steventon Rectory, in Hampshire, where six sons and two daughters were born to them, of whom Jane, born in 1775, was their seventh child. Bath faded into the background of the family concerns, though their relations kept them in touch with developments there. The city remained the home, for half each year at least, of Mrs Austen's brother and his wife; while her sister, Jane, who had married another clergyman, lived for a period in a village just outside Bath. It is not known how frequently the Austens visited either set of relations, or if they took their children with them. For 37 years the main business of their lives was to care for their farm and their parish, to educate and provide for their family, and to create in the Rectory the simple, healthy, happy and intellectually stimulating atmosphere in which all the children thrived, and the genius of one of them was nurtured.

By the time Jane Austen came intimately to know Bath, at around the turn of the century, her cheerful nature, inherited from her father and confirmed by a happy childhood in the country and in the bosom of a clever and affectionate family, was firmly established. Her judgement was mature, and her moral values were fixed. She brought to Bath an acute intelligence and a lively sense of the ridiculous and the pretentious. Bath was therefore not a formative influence upon her, but rather provided a wider sphere of observation, where she could measure manners and morals against ideas already formed.

Bath too had come to maturity while Jane was growing up at Steventon. 'Within the last fifty years', boasted the official guide of 1800, 'the city of Bath has so considerably increased in size and the number of its inhabitants, that it is become one of the *most agreeable* as well as *most polite* places in the kingdom; owing chiefly to the elegant neatness of its buildings, and the accommodations for strangers, which are superior to those of any city in Europe'.[3] The Royal Crescent, masterpiece of John Wood the younger, and perhaps the most beautiful terrace of houses in Europe, had been begun in the very year of Jane's birth, 1775.

Lansdown Crescent

9

Between 1780 and 1793 (in which year there was a financial slump caused by the war with France, and many builders went bankrupt) the number of houses in the city had increased by 45 per cent. By 1800 the boom was on again, and a whole new area of the city was being developed. There seemed no limit to the number of people aspiring to the good things Bath could offer. But they were a slightly different kind of people now. As Bath became attainable to greater numbers, so it lost its appeal for those at the top of the social pyramid, who forsook the city for newer spas and seaside resorts. But an increase in the population of Britain, and in the diffusion of prosperity and leisure, coupled with improvements in travel, ensured Bath's continuing popularity. With its excellent shops and medical and cultural amenities, it increasingly attracted residents as well as the many who still took a house for a few weeks during 'the season' (which lasted from October to May, but was at its height from January to March). The growing predominance of the middle classes, the new trend towards residence, and simply the different manners of a different age, all helped to give turn-of-the-century Bath the sedate and respectable character of a matron; she was no longer a flighty, giddy girl.

Jane Austen observed some of the later stages of this transformation for herself, and it has often been remarked with what accuracy and sensitivity the two portraits of the city given in *Northanger Abbey* and *Persuasion* reflect the social, moral and cultural changes which had taken place in the 17 or 18 years between the writing of these two novels, the first and last which she completed. The two portraits, both equally valid, also present two quite different functions of the city in terms of fiction. To Catherine Morland, Bath represents a pleasurable education; to Anne Elliot an unwelcome uprooting. Their different experiences are beautifully in tune with the different moods of the city which Jane Austen captures, evidence at once of her perfect mastery of her material, and her fidelity to real life.

Catherine Morland, comparing life in Bath with that in a country village, says, 'Here are a variety of amusements, a variety of things to be seen and done all day long, which I can know nothing of there'. The 'things to be seen and done' are explored in some detail in the chapters which follow.

Since this book is not a chronological jog through Jane Austen's life and work, even as it relates to Bath, but rather focusses, chapter by chapter, on the various aspects of the city which impinged on her, or about which she chose to write, it may be helpful here to say something about dates. The letters of Jane Austen from Bath which survive are confined to the periods May—June 1799; May—June 1801; January and April 1805.[4] There is also an interesting letter written by Mrs Austen from Bath in April 1806.[5] Sadly, nothing remains from the middle and most settled period of Jane's residence in the city. *Northanger Abbey* was written in 1798-99, and revised somewhat before 1803, in which year it was sold to a bookseller who promised to publish it, but who mysteriously failed to do so. Having bought the manuscript back many years later, Jane Austen prepared an apologetic notice in which she entreated the public 'to bear in mind that thirteen years have passed since it was finished, many more since it was begun, and that during that period, places, manners, books, and opinions have undergone considerable changes'. *Persuasion* was begun in 1815 and finished in July 1816. The two 'Bath' novels were published posthumously together in two volumes in December 1817.

From these sources I have taken all Jane Austen's references to Bath, and, amplifying them where necessary with explanations of contemporary customs, places and events, I have attempted to illuminate Bath for admirers of the novels; to provide a guide for exploring what remains (and it is a great deal) of the city Jane Austen knew; and to demonstrate its importance to her art. A novelist among whose aims and achievements was to catch the manners of an age, required to observe the full play of those manners in a public or civic setting as well as in domestic ones. Bath served better than London, both because Jane knew it more intimately, and because its *raison d'être* was to while away the leisure of the very classes of whom she wrote. And this is not to mention the moral dimension, which a place like Bath, so full of temptation to the frivolous or mercenary, enabled her pitilessly to examine and expose.

From Mrs Allen's simple praise, 'Bath is a charming place, sir', to Anne Elliot's silent disgust with 'the littlenesses of a town'; from Admiral Croft's hearty satisfaction in a place where he could be sure of meeting old friends, to Isabella Thorpe's affected cynicism, Bath evokes a wide variety of responses in Jane Austen's characters. The city is not only the backdrop to their doings, but very often the subject of their conversation. That is, it was more than merely a location, it was a social phenomenon, which interested her deeply as a novelist and as a woman. Her own attitude to the city was sometimes hostile, frequently ambivalent, yet the impression created by the complete body of her writings on the subject, as the following pages prove, is far from being a dismal one. I think this is partly because, as I have already suggested, her own temperament was sunny, and from habit and principle she always resolved to make the best of things. But partly this happy impression is left because however much Jane Austen might disapprove of the frivolous nature of some of Bath's pursuits, they were – if not taken too seriously – diverting, enjoyable, amusing. They gave her a unique opportunity for observing the ways of 'men and women': by her own confession, always her chief interest and delight. Bath existed for pleasure, and it needed someone much more sour-tempered or narrow-minded than Jane Austen, not to derive pleasure from it.

CHAPTER ONE

Arriving

The moment of arrival in Bath was one of great importance to Jane Austen, and to those of her characters who shared her heightened perceptions. Whether catching their first glimpses of the city with joyful anticipation or with a sinking heart, author and heroines were more than usually alert to the visual scene:

> They arrived in Bath. Catherine was all eager delight; – her eyes were here, there, everywhere, as they approached its fine and striking environs, and afterwards drove through those streets which conducted them to the hotel. She was come to be happy, and she felt happy already.

Catherine Morland's feelings, so natural to any young girl who has passed all her life in a country village, were probably those of Jane Austen herself the first time she holidayed in Bath. Though not so naïve as Catherine, and more accustomed to travel, Jane shared her youthful heroine's happy nature.[6] It is next to impossible that she did not relish all the new experiences offered by Bath, or look about with 'eager delight' at a place she had heard and read about so often.

Jane Austen's first known visit to Bath was in November 1797, when she was almost 22. Although no letters written during this visit survive, two or three references to it in the later correspondence establish it without a doubt. She would have had opportunities for visiting Bath before this, for her uncle and aunt, Mr and Mrs Leigh Perrot, kept a house in the Paragon as well as a country residence, and passed every winter of Jane's life in Bath, where Mr Leigh Perrot was thought to derive benefit from the waters. It would not be surprising, therefore, to find Jane staying with them periodically from an early age. Yet, nothing suggests that she did, while all the evidence points to the visit of 1797 being her first. She was inspired to begin *Northanger Abbey* soon after returning home.

On this visit Jane was accompanied by her mother and by her beloved sister, Cassandra, which is why no letters survive, for Cassandra was her principal correspondent whenever the sisters were separated by family visits. The following autumn, 1798,

1 The Paragon

Mrs Leigh Perrot sent a repeat invitation to her Austen relations.

'Tis really very kind of my Aunt to ask us to Bath again; a
kindness that deserves a better return than to profit by it

Jane wrote dryly to Cassandra, who was visiting their brother
Edward in Kent. Jane had detected symptoms of meanness in
her wealthy aunt, and was suggesting that Mrs Leigh Perrot
would regret her generosity in inviting them again so soon. Mrs
Leigh Perrot had many sterling qualities, as events were to prove;
and her husband was always kindness itself to his sister and her
family; but Jane was sensitive about being made to feel the poor
relation, under constant obligation to a snobbish, complaining
aunt she could not love.

From Kent, Cassandra reported that Edward's health was giving cause for concern. 'Poor Edward!' replied Jane. 'It is very
hard that he, who has everything in the world that he can wish
for, should not have good health too . . . I know no one more
deserving of happiness without alloy than Edward is.' But by the
following spring Edward still had not recovered, and he was
advised to see what the waters of Bath could do for him. With
his wife Elizabeth, daughter Fanny, aged six, and eldest son
Edward, five years old, (three younger sons were left at home in
the care of their nurse), Edward travelled to Steventon where he
collected his mother and younger sister, and they then proceeded
to Bath. Jane was therefore able to renew her acquaintance with
the city in more congenial company, and under circumstances of
greater independence, than a repeat visit to the Paragon.

They were no otherwise indebted to Mrs Leigh Perrot, probably, than for inspecting and booking their lodgings in advance.
The Austens took 13 Queen Square for a period of six weeks,
from 17 May to 27 June. The landlady was Mrs Bromley, who
according to the Guide of 1800 had lodgings to let at both 12 and
13 Queen Square. The travellers broke their journey from Hampshire to Bath in an inn at Devizes, in Wiltshire. From there it was
only half a day's journey to Bath. On arrival, Jane almost
immediately sat down to record her first impressions for Cassandra:

Well, here we are at Bath; we got here about one o'clock,
and have been arrived just long enough to go over the house,
fix on our rooms and be very well pleased with the whole
of it. Poor Elizabeth has had a dismal ride of it from Devizes,
for it has rained almost all the way, and our first view of
Bath has been just as gloomy as it was last November twelve-
month.

We stopped in Paragon as we came along, but as it was too wet and dirty for us to get out, we could only see Frank, who told us that his master was very indifferent, but had had a better night last night than usual.

We are exceedingly pleased with the house; the rooms are quite as large as expected. Mrs Bromley is a fat woman in mourning, and a little black kitten runs about the stair-case. Elizabeth has the apartment within the drawing-room; she wanted my mother to have it, but as there was no bed in the inner one, and the stairs are so much easier of ascent, or my mother so much stronger than in Paragon as not to regard the double flight, it is settled for us to be above, where we have two very nice-sized rooms . . .

I like our situation very much; it is far more cheerful than Paragon, and the prospect from the drawing-room window, at which I now write, is rather picturesque, as it commands a perspective view of the left side of Brock Street, broken by three Lombardy poplars in the garden of the last house in Queen's Parade.

Certainly Queen Square, with its open centre space, and views of distant gardens (it is the *backs* of the left side of Brock Street which can be seen from No. 13, in the south-west corner of the Square), is more airy and cheerful than the Paragon, a narrow street of tall houses on both sides, and taking all the London road traffic. Queen Square, begun in 1732, was as we have seen the earliest piece of town planning by John Wood, who wrote: 'For the Intention of a Square in a City is for People to assemble together; and the Spot whereon they meet, ought to be separated from the Ground common to Men and Beasts, and even to Man-kind in General, if Decency and good order are to be observed in such Places of Assembly'. By the time of Jane Austen's visit, this function had transferred itself to the Royal Crescent, where Sunday promenading was the custom, and Queen Square was no longer a particularly fashionable quarter of the town. Indeed, 17 years later still, when she came to write *Persuasion*, she could make the Miss Musgroves say, 'I hope we shall be in Bath this winter; but remember, papa, if we go, we must be in a good situation – none of your Queen-squares for us!'

To Jane Austen, looking out of the window of No. 13 in May 1799, the view was different in several respects from that of today. The Lombardy poplars have long gone, while the backs of the houses in Brock Street are almost wholly obscured by the trees which have grown up in their gardens. But more significantly,

13 Queen Square (with Beechen Cliff in the background)

the Square itself is altered. Now it too has its share of grass and trees; in 1799 it was still paved. Wood's plan for elegant parterres was never carried out, although the Guide of 1800 assured visitors that 'In this square is a pleasure ground encompassed by iron pallisades'. The west façade of the Square, now a complete run of building, was then interrupted in the centre, where a detached house belonging to the celebrated Dr Oliver was set back from the building line. On the corner just across the road from the window where Jane sat, was Wood's Queen Square Chapel, mentioned by her in a letter two years later. Unlike the Chapel, Queen's Parade, a terrace of twelve houses at an angle beyond the north-west corner of the Square, still stands. They were built by Wood on a piece of ground he had originally hoped to use for Assembly Rooms.

Mrs Austen retained a great affection for 'the Square' all her life ('My mother hankers after the Square dreadfully'), and its lack of fashion did not worry Jane Austen, who was not inclined to do justice to the Paragon. The Paragon indeed has its beauties – notably the view from the rear windows, where the land drops steeply away; beyond the rooftops of the immediate buildings distant prospects of the Avon valley and furthermost hills are quite dramatic. Because the rear of the Paragon, and that of its neighbour, Bladud Buildings, is so prominent a feature from the town, rearing up as they do cliff-like from the Walcot road, they are unique in Bath in having the fenestration of both façades symmetrically arranged. Mostly the backs of Georgian houses in Bath are an absolute hodge-podge, in comical contrast to the precision of their more public faces.

Jane's first two entrances into the city were made in gloomy weather. Her third approach to Bath was in an evening sun, though with some perversity she did not greatly prefer it. On Tuesday 5 May 1801 she wrote to Cassandra:

> The first view of Bath in fine weather does not answer my expectations; I think I see more distinctly through rain. The sun was got behind everything, and the appearance of the place from the top of Kingsdown was all vapour, shadow, smoke and confusion.

They were driving due west, and it was early evening. ('It was half after seven by your clocks before we entered the house.') Her unusually impressionistic description of the city under its pall of vapour and smoke (which, incidentally, oddly anticipates Dickens' description of Coketown on a fine day in *Hard Times*:

one does not often associate Bath with a northern city of the Industrial Revolution), not only confirms that this was the first occasion on which Jane had arrived in Bath when it was not raining, but gives a clue to the tenor of her mind at the time. She was approaching Bath reluctantly, and not just for a visit, but to make it her home.

Her situation she later transmuted to fiction in *Persuasion*, and her feelings were in accord with Anne Eliot's (though similarly kept to herself, for the sake of her companions). Jane makes Anne, too, arrive in the rain; it suits her mood. Anne, she wrote,

> persisted in a very determined, though very silent, disinclination for Bath; caught the first dim view of the extensive buildings, smoking in rain, without any wish of seeing them better; felt their progress through the streets to be, however disagreeable, yet too rapid.

Anne's companion in the carriage, Lady Russell, is susceptible to the sounds rather than the sights of the city. The two friends, though sympathetic to one another, differ sharply in their reactions to Bath. The older woman has recently suffered under the clamour of a houseful of children. The noises of Bath are much more to her taste, and, calm and sedate though she is, she hears them with a thrill of anticipation:

> When Lady Russell, not long afterwards, was entering Bath on a wet afternoon, and driving through the long course of streets from the Old Bridge to Camden-place, amidst the dash of other carriages, the heavy rumble of carts and drays, the bawling of newsmen, muffin-men and milkmen, and the ceaseless clink of pattens, she made no complaint. No, these were the noises which belonged to the winter pleasures; her spirits rose under their influence.

Unlike Catherine Morland, and Jane Austen herself, who always approached the city from Wiltshire, that is from the east, Lady Russell and Anne arrive from Somerset, the county in which Bath then occupied a northernmost corner. (Since 1974 Bath has belonged to a newly created county, Avon.) Anne's approach is therefore from the south, over the bridge which for centuries had been the only crossing of the river Avon at Bath. First built in 1362, complete with a tiny chapel dedicated to St Lawrence in the centre (where travellers could give thanks for a safe journey or pray for one on setting out) and defensive towers at the southern end, the Old Bridge had been rebuilt in 1754 without either of these memorials of a more precarious age, but with five very elegant arches spanning the Avon.

From the bridge on the southern boundary of the city to Camden Place (now known as Camden Crescent) in its 'lofty, dignified situation', as Jane Austen describes it, on the northern heights, is certainly 'a long course of streets', and a steep one too, rising from sea level to an altitude of some 84 metres. Later Anne was to find it a 'toilsome walk' to return home from the city centre; luckily she is often given a lift by Lady Russell. On this first entry into the city, 'She was put down in Camden-place; and Lady Russell then drove to her own lodgings, in Rivers-street'. Anne entered the house chosen by her father 'with a sinking heart, anticipating an imprisonment of many months, and anxiously saying to herself, "Oh! when shall I leave you again!"'

Jane Austen herself, entering Bath in much the same circumstances, had the further indignity of having to stay at the Paragon while a permanent home was sought. She and her mother arrived ahead of her father and Cassandra, and began house-hunting (the subject of the next chapter) straight away. Meanwhile the Leigh Perrots welcomed them warmly, and Jane, giving herself away only in her atmospheric description of the city, assured Cassandra 'I have the pleasure of writing from my *own* room up two pair of stairs, with everything very comfortable about me'. (Anticipating the stay at the Paragon, Jane had mischievously suggested she might try 'disordering my stomach with Bath buns' to avoid being too much drain on her aunt's housekeeping purse.)

Quite apart from the economic advantage of staying with relations while looking for a house, however, it was not at all usual for families to stay for any length of time at an hotel. Hotels and inns were used by single gentlemen, by families intending only a few days' stay – like the Musgroves, in *Persuasion*, who put up at the White Hart, where their suite of rooms included a 'handsome drawing room' where their friends could gather in private – and for taking meals. Hence the reference to 'the hotel' in the paragraph describing Catherine Morland's arrival. The fact that the Allens and Catherine Morland merely refreshed themselves at one of the Bath hotels before proceeding to the house which they had taken for their six or eight weeks' stay is evident from the next sentence, which assures us that 'They were soon settled in comfortable lodgings in Pulteney-street'.

The best families would take a whole house, people of lesser means half a house or one floor of rooms, in each case with a landlady to cook and serve their meals in their own dining room. 'The general price of lodgings from the first of September to the 31st May is 10s 6d a week for the best rooms, and 5s 6d for servant's rooms: the other three months, viz June, July and August, 7s 6d a week for the best rooms, and 5s 6d a week for the servant's rooms', the 1800 Guide informed prospective visitors. Food, which was purchased by the visitors according to their own wishes, was not included in these prices.

Amost certainly Catherine Morland's brother James, Isabella Thorpe's brother John, and Anne Elliot's cousin William all chose to stay in one of the hotels in Bath, since they were not travelling as part of a family which included females; certainly we are not given an address for any of them. (In *Pride and Prejudice*, the excuse given by Bingley's sisters for hastening after him to London, is so that he will not have to stay in a comfortless hotel.) The entrance of James Morland and John Thorpe into Bath rounds off our survey of arrivals; this one is seen through the eyes not of the arrivers, but of those to whom their coming is a delightful surprise. Catherine Morland and Isabella Thorpe have just left the Pump Room, walking as fast as they could in pursuit of two young men:

> Half a minute conducted them through the Pump-yard to the archway, opposite Union-passage; but here they were stopped. Everybody acquainted with Bath may remember the difficulties of crossing Cheap-street at this point; it is indeed a street of so impertinent a nature, so unfortunately connected with the great London and Oxford roads, and the principal inn of the city, that a day never passes in which parties of ladies, however important their business, whether in quest of pastry, millinery, or even (as in the present case) of young men, are not detained on one side or the other by carriages, horsemen, or carts. This evil had been felt and lamented, at least three times a day, by Isabella since her residence in Bath; and she was now fated to feel and lament it once more, for at the very moment of their coming opposite to Union-passage, and within view of the two gentlemen who were proceeding through the crowds, and threading the gutters of that interesting alley, they were prevented crossing by the approach of a gig, driven along on bad pavement by a most knowing-looking coachman with all the vehemence that could most fitly endanger the lives of himself, his companion, and his horse.
>
> 'Oh these odious gigs!' said Isabella, looking up, 'how I detest them.' But this detestation, though so just, was of short duration, for she looked again and exclaimed, 'Delightful! Mr Morland and my brother!'
>
> 'Good heaven! 'tis James!' was uttered at the same moment by Catherine.

Undoubtedy the destination of Thorpe and Morland was 'the principal inn of the city', The Bear, which was so near to Union Passage that its yard stood for many years in the way of making a proper carriage road through to the top of the town. Ten years after it had been planned and longer still since the desperate need of such a road had been felt, Union Street was built at last in 1807, parallel to Union Passage, and it figures in *Persuasion*. Since on meeting the young ladies John Thorpe hands his equipage over to a servant, with instructions about his horse, it is evident that they had almost reached their destination. I think, therefore, that we can picture Thorpe and Morland residing at The Bear, roughing it as suits dashing young men, while their respective sisters enjoy the greater comfort and gentility of private lodgings.

There is one last thing to say on the subject of arriving. 'Let us go and look at the arrivals,' says Isabella in the Pump Room and 'Away they walked to the book', where Isabella busies herself examining the names inscribed therein. Later, Catherine finds out at which number in Milsom Street the Tilneys have their lodgings by consulting the same book. 'An order of 1787' decreed 'That ladies and gentlemen coming to town, give orders that their names and places of abode be entered in any of the Pump-Room books; and the Master of Ceremonies thus publickly requests the favour of such Ladies and Gentlemen, to whom he has not the honour of being personally known, to offer him some favourable occasion of being presented to them, that he may be enabled to shew that attention, which is not more his duty than his inclination to observe.' This notice, signed by James King, Master of Ceremonies at the Lower Rooms, was inserted regularly in the Bath Guide Books, including that of 1800. (Mr King is named as the man who introduces Henry Tilney to Catherine, at her first dance at the Lower Rooms.) 'Places of abode' presumably refers to the address in Bath rather than at home, or Catherine would have discovered when she consulted the book that the Tilneys had the great happiness to live in an Abbey.

For those who did not care to be seen being nosy in public, the same information (but without 'places of abode') could be obtained from one of the two local weekly papers, the *Bath Chronicle*, which each week carried a list of new arrivals. 'I will get the Bath paper and look over the new arrivals', says Henry Tilney at Northanger, while in *Persuasion* Sir Walter Elliot is thrown into a quiver when 'The Bath paper one morning announced the arrival of the Dowager Viscountess Dalrymple, and her daughter, the Honourable Miss Carteret'.

The *Bath Chronicle* for Thursday 23 May 1799 includes among the new arrivals for that week, 'Mr and Mrs E Austin' [sic]. This presumably refers to Edward and Elizabeth, a couple wealthy enough (since Edward had been made heir of a distant relation, Mr Knight) to deserve mention. In neither May 1799, nor May 1801, however, does the newspaper announce the arrival of that insignificant person, Miss Jane Austen.

CHAPTER TWO

House-Hunting

When, in December 1800, Jane Austen was told by her parents that they had suddenly decided to leave the country rectory where she had lived all her life, and retire to Bath, she is said to have fainted with shock. In accordance with her principles, however, she soon taught herself to make the best of the situation which she could not alter. Her parents had worked hard for 37 years; her father was growing infirm, her mother was, or fancied herself, ill, and both deserved rest from the cares of parish, farm and a household which produced, with incessant labour, almost every item it consumed. In Bath provisions could be bought at market; social life could be easily enjoyed; and every amenity for procuring health and for whiling away leisure hours was on hand. Moreover, Bath was endeared to her parents from being the scene of their courtship, and the residence of Mr Leigh Perrot. All this was very reasonable, and must be borne with cheerfulness by dutiful daughters – who, however much they might prefer a country life themselves, at 25 and 28 had no option but to accompany their parents to Bath.

The idea of retiring to Bath had perhaps been put into their heads by a distant relation, on Mrs Austen's side, doing the same. 'My mother has heard from Mrs E Leigh. Lady S & S [Saye and Sele] and her daughter are going to remove to Bath', Jane had written, perfectly unsuspicious of what was to follow, on 20 November 1800. It seems probable that it was this piece of news which set Mr and Mrs Austen thinking, although of course they had the example of Mrs Austen's own father retiring to Bath 40 years before. But that no such move had been in their minds before the letter from Mrs Leigh seems evident from the fact that in the very same month alterations were being made to the garden at Steventon, and some new furniture purchased for the Rectory, which could not be taken with them to Bath.

The plan was to leave Steventon in May 1801, and stay at the Paragon while they looked for a house of their own. Knowing Bath well, the Austens began to think about where they would like the house to be while they were still at Steventon. Cassandra was on another long visit to Edward when the decision to move to Bath was made, and in a letter of 3 January, when the sisters had begun to come to terms with the change in their lives, Jane sent her first recorded thoughts on the subject of house-hunting.

There are three parts of Bath which we have thought of as likely to have Houses in them – Westgate Buildings, Charles Street, & some of the short streets leading from Laura Place or Pulteney Street: Westgate Buildings, tho' quite in the lower part of the Town are not badly situated in themselves; the street is broad, & has rather a good appearance. Charles Street however I think is preferable; the buildings are new, & its nearness to Kingsmead fields would be a pleasant circumstance. – Perhaps you may remember, or perhaps you may forget that Charles Street leads from the Queen Square Chapel to the two Green Park-streets. The Houses in the streets near Laura Place I should expect to be above our price. – Gay Street would be too high, except only the lower house on the left hand side as you ascend; towards *that* my Mother has no disinclination; – it used to be lower rented than any other house in the row, from some inferiority in the apartments. But above all others, her wishes are at present fixed on the corner house in Chapel row, which opens into Prince's Street. Her knowledge of it however is confined to the outside, & therefore she is equally uncertain of its being really desirable as of its being to be had. In the meantime she assures you that she will do everything in her power to avoid Trim Street altho' you have not expressed the fearful presentiment of it, which was rather expected. – We know that Mrs Perrot will want to get us into Axford Buildings, but we all unite in a particular dislike of that part of the Town, & therefore hope to escape. Upon these different situations, You and Edward may confer together, & your opinion of each will be expected with eagerness.

Westgate Buildings, erected on the line of the south-west section of the old borough walls, was among the earliest developments in Bath. The Corporation had agreed to demolish part of the wall to make way for it, the first part of the wall to go. The erection of Westgate Buildings, ironically, cut off the views over the fields beyond the city walls which had been enjoyed by the very first houses built for visitors, by Jane Austen's ancestor, the Duke of Chandos.

This lower part of the town could never compete for salubriousness and desirability with the northern slopes. It was too low-lying, too close to the river, and too much associated with the arc of slums which curved round the southern end of the town and which housed the majority of the artisans on whose labour the comfortable lives of the visitors and leisured residents depended. This compressed area had the highest number of alehouses and noxious workshops per acre of any in the city, not to mention the greatest concentration of prostitutes, beggars and thieves. No wonder that arch-snob Sir Walter Elliot should reproach Anne for visiting an old friend, living in this quarter in reduced circumstances, occupying 'a noisy parlour, and a dark bedroom behind'. 'Westgate-buildings!' said he; 'and who is Miss Anne Elliot to be visiting in Westgate-buildings?' and, not letting the matter drop, 'Westgate-buildings must have been rather surprised by the appearance of a carriage drawn up near its pavement!'

'Gay Street would be too high', might mean too expensive, or too elevated – I think the latter. With Mr and Mrs Austen both growing frail – by 1804 Mr Austen could walk only with the aid of a stick – they were sensible in avoiding too much climbing of hills, which ruled out many of the more open and delightful of locations. Axford Buildings, which the Austens were anxious to escape, was a continuation of the Paragon, and quite as high as Gay Street. Mr and Mrs Austen appear to have considered only streets fairly level with the city centre, whether they be to the west and south of Queen Square, where prices were moderate, or to the east of the city of the new and fashionable Bathwick estate, the numerous advantages of which included a level approach to the city centre.

To the east, Bath had stopped short at the River Avon long after it had begun to spread in all other directions, until the owner of the 600 acres of the Bathwick manor, on the other side of the river, was entrepreneurial enough to build a bridge and open up his land for development. Pulteney Bridge, the work of Robert Adam; Laura Place, the diamond-shaped enclosure into which it issued; Great Pulteney Street, the broad and noble thoroughfare leading from Laura Place; and Sydney Gardens, which closed the whole magnificent vista, are among the late 18th century glories of Bath. The first stone of Laura Place had not been laid until March 1788. Jane's next letter to Cassandra again discussed the relative merits of Westgate Buildings and Laura Place:

Miss Lyford [a Steventon neighbour] was very pleasant, and gave my mother such an account of the houses in Westgate Buildings, where Mrs Lyford lodged four years ago, as made her think of a situation there with great pleasure; but your opposition will be without difficulty, decisive, & my father in particular who was very well inclined towards the Row before, has now ceased to think of it entirely. – At present the Environs of Laura Place seem to be his choice. His views on the subject are much advanced since I came home; he

Reflections of Laura Place

grows quite ambitious & actually requires now a comfortable
and creditable looking house.

It is not known how much the Austens were prepared to pay
for a house; they had, of course, always lived rent-free before.
On his retirement Mr Austen remained nominally Rector of
Steventon, his duties being taken over by his eldest son, James,
who moved with his family into the Rectory. Mr Austen, however,
was entitled to keep a proportion of the stipend, and he and his
wife had besides some small investments. Both had inherited a
little property from their parents.[7] Their total annual income
when they moved to Bath was about £600. This may be compared
with the known rental of a house in Laura Place in 1792 – a
house which had the unusual advantage of two water closets –
of £120. As Jane wrote in *Persuasion*, 'Lady Dalrymple had taken
a house, for three months, in Laura-place, and would be living
in style'.

As for the size of the house required by the Austens, it was to be home for only four people, and Jane and Cassandra were accustomed and happy to share a bedroom. Naturally they wanted space enough for brothers and their families occasionally to visit them. The Austens planned to keep a cook, a housemaid and a manservant in Bath; these would of course sleep in the garrets. It is not to be supposed that the Austens intended to hold large parties, give grand dinners, or appear to be 'established with all the credit and dignity' which Sir Walter Elliot found so indispensable. (But even he 'gave no dinners in general' lest his reduced circumstances be betrayed.)

But everyone likes a good house, and a good situation. Having received Cassandra's reply, Jane wrote a week later:

> I join with you in wishing for the Environs of Laura Place, but do not venture to expect it. – My mother hankers after the Square dreadfully, & it is but natural to suppose that my Uncle will take *her* part. – It would be very pleasant to be near Sidney Gardens! – we might go into the Labyrinth every day.

Early in May, Jane and her mother arrived at the Paragon, to be joined a month later by Mr Austen and Cassandra, who were paying separate family visits. Again therefore, Jane took up the subject of house-hunting in her letters to Cassandra, keeping her well informed of every possibility. On the morning after their arrival Jane wrote: 'I fancy we are to have a house in Seymour Street, or thereabouts. My uncle and aunt both like that situation. I was glad to hear the former talk of all the houses in New King Street as too small; it was my own idea of them'. A week later, however, they had the opportunity to examine a house in Seymour Street, and found it not as suitable as the Leigh Perrots had imagined:

> Yesterday morning we looked into a house in Seymour Street which there is reason to suppose will soon be empty, and as we are assured from many quarters that no inconvenience from the river is felt in those Buildings, we are at liberty to fix in them if we can; but this house was not inviting; the largest room downstairs, was not much more than fourteen feet square, with a western aspect.

A quest to New King Street, as Jane had supposed, proved equally fruitless:

> I went with my mother to help look at some houses in New

King Street, towards which she felt some kind of inclination, – but their size has now satisfied her – they were smaller than I expected to find them. One in particular out of the two, was quite monstrously little; the best of the sittingrooms not so large as the parlour at Steventon, – and the second room in every floor about capacious enough to admit a very small single bed.

There was a worse disappointment with another location: Green Park Buildings, also down by the river, consisted of two rows of houses jutting at angles into Kingsmead meadows. They had been built less than two years, on land which regularly flooded, though in an effort to counteract this the houses were raised up on a platform of vaults. The situation was extremely pleasant, with a triangular garden between the two rows, the third side of the triangle being formed by the river. On the evening on 5 May Jane wrote:

> When my uncle went to take his second glass of water I walked with him, and in our morning's circuit we looked at two houses in Green Park Buildings, one of which pleased me very well. We walked all over it except into the garrets; the dining-room is of a comfortable size, just as large as you like to fancy it; the second room about 14ft square. The apartment over the drawing-rooom pleased me particularly, because it is divided into two, the smaller one a very nice-sized dressing-room, which upon occcasion might admit a bed. The aspect is south-east. The only doubt is about the dampness of the offices, of which there were symptoms.

But by 21 May:

> Our views of G.P. Buildings seem all at an end; the observation of the damp still remaining in the offices of a house which has only been vacated a week, with reports of discontented families & putrid fevers, has given the *coup de grâce*. – We have now nothing in view. – When you arrive, we will at least have the pleasure of examining some of these putrifying houses again; – they are so very desirable in size and situation, that there is some satisfaction in spending ten minutes within them.

Finally, On May 26, Jane wrote to Cassandra:

> Mrs Evelyn called very civilly on Sunday, to tell us that Mr Evelyn had seen Mr Philips the proprietor of No. 12 G.P.B. and that Mr Philips was very willing to raise the kitchen

27 Green Park Buildings

floor; – but all this I fear is fruitless – tho' the water may be kept out of sight, it cannot be sent away, nor the ill effects of its nearness be excluded. I have nothing more to say on the subject of houses; except that we were mistaken as to the aspect of the one in Seymour Street, which instead of being due west is north-west.

Jane's weariness with the subject is evident; and since Cassandra and Mr Austen now arrived at the Paragon, no more letters exist to tell of how a house was found at last. The dampness of the area Mrs Austen had favoured, the smallness of the houses they had examined within their price range, presumably enabled Mr. Austen's original wishes to prevail, and Bathwick was again considered. Perhaps they decided it was worth paying a little more for a house they would be happy and healthy in; perhaps Mr Austen was more optimistic, less cautious, about money matters than his wife, and on his arrival in Bath his optimism won the others over. They must all have been attracted by the advertisement appearing in the local paper for three and a quarter years' lease on 4 Sydney Place: 'The situation is desirable, the Rent very low and the Landlord is bound by Contract to paint the first two floors this summer'.

It was not exactly 'the Environs of Laura Place', but something not far off, and equally 'comfortable and creditable', that they gained. Sydney Place is set at an angle to the end of Great Pulteney Street: rather a long walk into town, but a perfectly level one. But the chief glory of Sydney Place is that it immediately overlooks Sydney Gardens: all the Austens' principal rooms gave a view of greenery. In 1801 the terrace was only nine years old. It had been designed by Thomas Baldwin, the City Architect who had also designed the magnificent Great Pulteney Street and made street plans for the whole of Bathwick meadows, but who had gone bankrupt in the crash of '97. The rear of Sydney Place overlooked these still undeveloped meadows in 1801; Daniel Street, which was intended to run behind Sydney Place, was not built until 1810, and many of Baldwin's streets never materialized at all. In 1801, Sydney Place must have felt quite like the country, and Jane must have felt happy with her parents' choice – unless niggling financial worry robbed her of her satisfaction.

Since this was to be Jane Austen's principal home in Bath, the only one in which the family were properly settled, and the only one now to bear a plaque proclaiming her name, and since the house was and is architecturally such a good one, it is worth quoting the description of it from Walter Ison's *The Georgian*

Baldwin planned Sydney Place with eight terraces of houses fronting on to the road surrounding the hexagonal pleasure gardens, but only the range on the west side, lying between Great Pulteney and Bathwick Streets was built to his designs.

The fourteen houses are grouped to form a balanced composition, with slightly projecting pavilions at each end and in the centre. The division into three stories is strongly defined by the plinth below the first-floor windows, the plain sill underlining the second-floor windows, and the simple crowning entablature. On the ground-storey arched doorways, dressed with vermiculated rustications, form every third opening from either end, meeting to form a pair in the central pavilion. The windows are set in groups of three to each house and generally have plain surroundings, but decorative interest is provided at first-floor level by the elaborate setting of the middle windows in each pavilion, and those above the doorways to the intermediate houses. In each of these last the window is framed within a moulded architrave, surmounted by a plain frieze and cornice, and flanked by half-pilasters with plain shafts and composite capitals lining up with the frieze.[8]

The Austens took No. 4 from Michaelmas Day, and then went off for several weeks to enjoy a holiday by the sea, while the landlord fulfilled his contract to decorate. This is confirmed by a letter which Eliza Austen, first cousin and wife to Jane's brother Henry, wrote to a mutual relation, Philadelphia Walter, on 29 October 1801:

I conclude that you know of our uncle and aunt Austen & their daughters having spent the summer in Devonshire. They are now returned to Bath where they are superintending the fitting up of their new house.

The only furniture which the family brought with them from Steventon were their beds. All the rest was sold at auction, and replacements bought in Bath, where there was an excellent choice. 'I flatter myself that for little comforts of all kinds, our apartment will be one of the most complete things of the sort all over Bath – Bristol included', Jane had written from Steventon. 'My mother bargains for having no trouble at all in furnishing our house in Bath.' It was cheaper to do this than to transport what they owned already over such a distance. It will be remembered that Marianne Dashwood's pianoforte, and other household effects of the Dash-

4 Sydney Place

wood family, which had to be moved from Sussex to Devon, were 'sent round by water', which gives some idea of the state of the roads. Similarly, when the Brontë sisters' parents married in 1812, their mother's books and clothes were sent from Penzance to Yorkshire by sea, where they were unfortunately lost by shipwreck.

Jane's own piano, incidentally, was sold, and if she had a replacement, then it was hired, as happened later when she lived at Southampton. It was not until she was once more settled in a country village that she again purchased a piano. Playing the piano, mechanically, in the early morning before anybody else was up, was, I believe, an aid to composition for Jane Austen, rather than a musical indulgence; it enabled her mind to float free, and to inhabit the world of her creation, calling up scenes and conversations that would be committed to paper later in the day. If I am right, then the lack of a piano would have contributed to her failure to write very much in her Bath years, a failure which is often attributed to a disruptive social life, or to various personal sorrows.

The Austens remained three years at Sydney Place (each summer leaving Bath for a long holiday on the south coast), but no letters survive from this address, presumably because Jane and Cassandra were never parted. At the end of the three years, they moved. Perhaps the rent was becoming too great a burden; there seems no other reason why they should disrupt themselves and begin the task of house-hunting all over again. A family called Cole took 4 Sydney Place, putting their 'infamous' name-plate on the door, to Jane's chagrin. The Austens took themselves off to Green Park Buildings, the subject of so much discussion three years earlier. In other words they settled for economy, with some risk of damp.

Within three months of the move to Green Park Buildings, Mr Austen died, in January 1805. He was 73. Jane's brothers rallied round. James and his wife Mary, she wrote to Frank, at sea, 'kindly press my Mother to remove to Steventon as soon as it is all over, but I do not believe she will leave Bath at present. We must have this house for three months longer, & here we shall probably stay till the end of that time.'

Henry also wrote to Frank in the same strain:

> Yours reached me yesterday soon after my return from Walcot Church where in company with James I saw deposited the remains of the best of Fathers, and Men . . . . I believe that my Mother [will] remain in this house till Lady Day, & then probably reduce her establishment to one female

domestic & take furnished lodgings. She does not like to leave Bath altogether so long as Mr Perrot continues here & seems to derive comfort from her society.

The brothers all agreed to contribute to the keep of their mother and sisters, and made up Mrs Austen's remaining income of £140 to £450 per annum. Three days after Henry's letter, James too wrote to Frank, 'Her future plans are not quite settled, but I believe her summers will be spent in the country amongst her relations & chiefly I trust among her children – the winters she will pass in comfortable lodgings in Bath'.

Their income reduced, and their household likewise, to four people instead of seven (including servants), the Austens now needed only half a house. When the lease of Green Park Buildings expired on Lady Day, they moved to Gay Street, a good situation in itself – well above the damps, and not far from the Leigh Perrots. Gay Street even had Sir Walter Elliot's approval: 'The Crofts had placed themselves in lodgings in Gay-street, perfectly to Sir Walter's satisfaction'. From this address Jane wrote in April to Cassandra: 'Mr Hampson is here'. (He was a distant relation on her father's side.) 'I met him the other morning in his way (as he said) to Green Park Buildings; I trusted to his forgetting our number in Gay Street when I gave it him, & so I conclude he has, as he [has] not yet called.'

Perhaps Gay Street also proved too expensive, as when next we hear of the Austens they are at 'Trim Street still', according to the address on Mrs Austen's letter to her daughter-in-law Mary, written on 10 April 1806. Trim Street, though in Mrs Austen's favourite vicinity of Queen Square, is cramped and narrow, without architectural distinction, a very early extension of Bath beyond the city walls. Yet again they were house-hunting, and now considering a move quite to the top of the town.

> We are disappointed of the lodgings in St James's Square; a person is in treaty for the whole house, so of course he will be prefer'd to us who want only a part. We have looked at some others since, but don't quite like the situation – hope a few days hence we shall have more choice, as it is supposed many will be quitting Bath when this gay week is over.

In fact, the Austens themselves were soon to quit Bath, for good, and quite unexpectedly, when a new plan suddenly presented itself. But that part of their story remains to be told in another chapter.

25 Gay Street

The importance of a good address is given more weight in *Persuasion* than in *Northanger Abbey*, where the only comment on the subject is Mrs Allen's on General Tilney, right at the end of the book: 'His lodgings were taken the very day after he left them, Catherine. But no wonder; Milsom-street, you know'. Evidently Henry had done his job well; it will be remembered that when Catherine first met him, he was in Bath 'to engage lodgings', as she afterwards learned from Eleanor. But even the General cannot match Sir Walter Elliot for snobbery, and *Persuasion* is suffused by value judgments of this kind. We have already heard Sir Walter's estimation of Westgate Buildings, Laura Place and Gay Street. He was ready to admit Colonel Wallis as an acquaintance, because his wife is said to be very pretty and because he is 'living in very good style in Marlborough Buildings'. At right-angles to and overlooking the Royal Crescent, and with open views to the west from the rear where the old Town Commons could not be built on, Marlborough Buildings was indeed a very good situation.

But Sir Walter thought he had an even better himself. 'Sir Walter had taken a very good house in Camden-place, a lofty, dignified situation, such as becomes a man of consequence; and both he and Elizabeth were settled there, much to their satisfaction.' The building (later known as Camden Crescent) was named after Charles Pratt, Marquis of Camden, politician and Recorder of Bath, whose crest, an elephant's head, adorns the keystones above each door. The central pediment, which because the crescent was never finished ended up disconcertingly off-centre, carries his coat of arms and perhaps marks the very house of the Elliots, since we are told that 'Their house was undoubtedly the best in Camden-place. Everybody was wanting to visit them.' In this house Anne marvelled to see Elizabeth, who had once been mistress of Kellynch Hall, throw open the double doors between the two principal apartments, and glory in walls 'perhaps thirty feet assunder'.

The location chosen for the Elliots by Jane Austen suits them to perfection, reflecting as it does not only their hauteur and pretentiousness, but the shaky ground on which these were built. To quote Walter Ison again:

> Camden Crescent forms only part of a large unfinished project begun round about 1788 on the south-east slope of Beacon Hill. On this site, with its magnificent and airy prospect, the promoters intended to build a great crescent with wings, forming Upper Camden Place, having before it a large garden sloping towards a terrace of houses, and Lower Camden

Camden Crescent

Place, forming a tangent to the crescent. The site was cleared and levelled at considerable expense and rapid progress had been made with the building of the upper crescent, when a series of alarming landslips brought the work to a standstill. That part of the building which was sited on solid rock was completed, but no further progress was made with the remaining houses, which were eventually demolished. For some years the north-east pavilion of the crescent remained as an isolated and picturesque ruin perched on a crag of rock, and can be seen as such in the drawings of Nattes and others. [It was highly visible from the Paragon.]

Upper Camden Place, now Camden Crescent, was originally planned to consist of thirty-two houses, of which twenty-two were to form the crescent proper, with its great Corinthian order, the remainder composing the flanking wings, their simply treated elevations being stepped down to overcome the sharp falls in the ground level. Because of the landslip only eighteen houses of the crescent, together with the whole of the left wing, were completed, so that the pedimented centre has only four houses on its right, but even in this truncated state Camden Crescent forms a beautiful and impressive landmark in any prospect of Bath from the east.[9]

The amount of time spent by Jane Austen in house-hunting and discussing various locations in Bath, bore fruit when she came to place all her characters at appropriate addresses; but the choice of Camden Crescent, with its subtle yet glorious symbolism, for Sir Walter Elliot, is surely unsurpassed.

CHAPTER THREE

Taking the Waters

Falling as rain on the Mendip hills some ten thousand years before, seeping slowly down to be warmed by the natural heat of the earth's core, the thermal springs which rise swiftly under pressure through faults in the rock to surface where the city of Bath now stands, were the prime reason for its development as a health resort by both the Romans and the Georgians.

Whatever other attractions drew visitors to Bath through the course of the 18th century, it was in quest of a cure for their many ailments that they first came, and that they continued to come in great measure even in Jane Austen's day. 'It will be too tedious at present', says the Bath Guide of 1800, 'to enumerate all the diseases curable by Bath Water, internally taken or externally used. Many people have come to Bath, tired with taking medicines (at home) to no manner of purpose at all; they have drank the Bath water with abundance of delight and pleasure, and by the help of a little physic have recovered to admiration.'

In histories of the city it has become a commonplace to assert that, with most people, health very soon became a mere pretext, and that society and amusement were what they really sought from Bath. But it is notable how many of Jane Austen's characters, as well as of her acquaintance, who came to Bath did so primarily to take the waters. In an age which could offer little else by way of alleviation, Bath was still resorted to in hope by sufferers real and imaginary, rich or poor, dying or merely slightly less than well.

It was often friends and relations of the invalid who found themselves provided with a fine excuse for a few weeks in Bath, and who swelled the ranks of the idle pleasure-seekers. Thus when Mr Allen 'was ordered to Bath for the benefit of a gouty constitution' both his wife and Catherine Morland enjoy the advantages of a holiday there. Mrs Allen, who is of all Jane Austen's characters perhaps the greatest enthusiast for Bath, discusses her husband's health very comfortably with Henry Tilney on that young man's return to the city:

> 'Well, sir, and I dare say you are not sorry to be back again, for it is just the place for young people – and indeed for everybody else too. I tell Mr Allen, when he talks of being sick of it, that I am sure he should not complain, for it is so very agreeable a place, that it is much better to be here

than at home at this dull time of year. I tell him he is quite in luck to be sent here for his health.'

'And I hope, madam, that Mr Allen will be obliged to like the place, from finding it of service to him.'

'Thank you, sir. I have no doubt that he will. – A neighbour of ours, Dr Skinner, was here for his health last winter, and came away quite stout.'

'That circumstance must give great encouragement.'

'Yes, sir – and Dr Skinner and his family were here three months; so I tell Mr Allen he must not be in a hurry to get away.'

The Allens lengthen their stay in Bath from six to eight weeks, but we do not hear whether Mr Allen derives any lasting benefit from the waters. His wife has nothing to say on that very material point when she meets Catherine Morland again at Fullerton. Mrs Allen's recollection of Bath centres on gowns and gloves, while Catherine is still too preoccupied with General Tilney's dreadful treatment of her to make the polite enquiry.

General Tilney too is in Bath to drink the waters, as Eleanor explains:

> My father can seldom be prevailed upon to give the waters what I think a fair trial. He has been disappointed of some friends' arrival whom he expected to meet here, and as he is now pretty well, is in a hurry to get home.

Another character sent to Bath because he was 'thought to be gouty' is Admiral Croft, in *Persuasion*. ('Gout and decrepitude!' exclaims Sir Walter in disgust when he hears the news.) Sir Walter might perhaps scorn to drink the waters, but even characters who do not appear to be ill do so, to make the most of their being in Bath, perhaps. Thus Lady Russell is described as being vexed by Mrs Clay's presence 'as much as a person in Bath who drinks the water, gets all the new publications and has a very large acquaintance has time to be vexed'.

Mention of visiting Bath for health is not confined to the 'Bath' novels. In the short novel in letters, *Lady Susan*, Mrs Johnson exultantly tells her friend Lady Susan that her husband 'is going for his health to Bath, where if the waters are favourable to his constitution & my wishes, he will be laid up with the gout many weeks'. (She adds 'Three years ago when *I* had a fancy for Bath, nothing could induce him to have a gouty symptom'.) Mr Woodhouse, in *Emma*, had tried the waters 'more than once, formerly; but without receiving any benefit', as his daughter tells Mrs Elton. That lady, who is proud of having lived much in Bath, is as convinced that the waters must be of use to Mr

Woodhouse's health, as the cheerfulness of the place to his spirits. 'I assure you, Miss Woodhouse, where the waters do agree it is quite wonderful the relief they give. In my Bath life, I have seen such instances of it!' Later in the novel, she recommends Bath for the ailing Mrs Churchill.

Jane Austen's uncle James Leigh Perrot was one who certainly believed in the efficacy of the waters. He evidently drank from the pump twice a day, since she mentions walking out with him 'when my uncle went to take his second glass of water'. A confirmed invalid in his habits, though he lived to be over 80, he arranged his whole life around this dependence on Bath water, forsaking the mansion in the country which he had built himself and which he professed to love, in order to spend at least half of each year in Bath.

The Bath Guide advises:

> The water should always be drank hot from the pump, or else at your lodgings as warm as it can possibly be procured . . . . The water is generally drank in the morning fasting, between the hours of six and ten, that it may have time to pass out of the stomach; though some drink a glass about noon. The quantity generally taken in a day is from one pint to three, though some drink two quarts; few constitutions require more.

The thermal water rises in three locations within the old city walls, and since mediaeval times had been collected into the Hot Bath, the King's Bath and the Cross Bath, all rebuilt during the 18th century, and each having an associated pump. That attached to the Hot Bath was known as the Hetling Pump, after a wine merchant who once owned the site. In each location the water surfaces at a constant temperature: in the Hot Bath at 49°C, in the King's Bath at 46°C, and in the Cross Bath at 40°C. The King's Bath, closest to the Abbey, was always the most favoured of the three, and here the finest Pump Room was built in 1706, and enlarged and remodelled in the last decade of the 18th century. The pumps at the other sites were merely for drinking the waters; the Pump Room opening onto the Abbey Churchyard was a social meeting place as well.

'The Nobility and Gentry assemble in it every morning, between the hours of seven and ten, to drink the water; for whose entertainment a good band of musick attends during the season', declares the 1800 Bath Guide. In describing the typical visitor's day elsewhere in its pages it asserts 'In the morning, the rendez-vous is at the Pump-Room; – from that time till noon in walking on

The Pump Room

the Parades, or in the different quarters of the town; thence to the Pump-Room again, and after a fresh stroll, to dinner'.

Mr Allen is one of those who drink about noon; on the morning when Catherine watches anxiously at the window for the rain to cease, so that she may go walking with the Tilneys, Mr Allen sets off for the Pump Room between twelve-thirty and one o'clock, though 'it was too dirty for Mrs Allen to accompany her husband'. Rain never keeps Mr Allen from the Pump Room, but on fine days he is accompanied by his wife and Catherine, leaving them to saunter and gossip while he seeks masculine company. 'Mr Allen after drinking his glass of water, joined some gentlemen to talk over the politics of the day and compare the accounts of their newspapers'.

It is the constant habit in *Northanger Abbey* to set off for the Pump Room at about one o'clock. That is the hour when Catherine and Isabella 'meet by appointment'. On another occasion Catherine resolves to read her book until one o'clock and then go in search of her new friend Eleanor Tilney, since 'in the Pump Room one so newly arrived must be met with'. She has already found that building excellent for the discovery of female friendship, and Isabella frequently appropriates it for her favourite pastime of flirtation.

The Hot Bath and the Cross Bath were close to one another, and situated in a less elegant part of the old walled town, the south-west quarter. Until the end of the eighteenth century this area retained its muddled mediaeval street-plan, but in 1789 an Act was passed to modernize the area, and five new streets were cut through. These included the very beautiful Bath Street, with its segmental ends, and colonnaded ranks of shops affording a sheltered walkway between the two groups of baths.

Grave invalids not only drank the water, of course, but bathed in it. The only such character in Jane Austen's work is Mrs Smith, in *Persuasion*. She was:

> afflicted with a severe rheumatic fever, which finally settling in her legs, had made her for the present a cripple. She had come to Bath on that account, and was now in lodgings near the hot-baths, living in a very humble way, unable to afford herself the comfort of a servant, and of course almost excluded from society.

We also learn that Mrs Smith 'never quitted the house but to be conveyed into the warm bath'. At one point it seems to be suggested that she visited the bath by evening, but this was

The Hot Bath

certainly not the fashionable hour. Perhaps some sort of segregation was in operation. The Bath Guide advised visitors of quality:

> The time for bathing is in the morning fasting at all times of the year; because, being refreshed by a night's sleep, we are better able to bear bathing . . . . You may drink a glass or two of the water during the time you are in the bath, it being very refreshing; and not only quenches thirst, but also promotes perspiration after. – The time of staying in the bath must be regulated by the physician or apothecary, according to the patient's strength or disorder.

With its concentration of invalids, most of them a good deal wealthier than Mrs Smith, Bath was obviously an excellent place to establish a medical practice. The Bath Guide of 1800 names 18 surgeons, 23 physicians, 28 apothecaries and 'chymists', and 4 dentists (a profession which had not figured in the guide 10 years before). In her letters Jane Austen mentions several of these men by name. In May 1799, when Edward Austen came to Bath for the sake of his health, he put himself under the care of Dr Fellowes, whom the Guide describes as Physician Extraordinary to the Prince of Wales. Dr Fellowes' address is given as 4 Bladud Buildings, which made him a very near neighbour of the Leigh Perrots, yet it does not seem to have been they who recommended him. As Jane mentions at one point going to the theatre with Mrs Fellowes, it is possible that the families were already known to one another socially, perhaps through some of Edward's connections in Kent.

About a fortnight after the Austens arrived, on Sunday 2 June, Jane reported on Edward's health to Cassandra:

> He was better yesterday than he had been for two or three days before, about as well as while he was at Steventon. – He drinks at the Hetling Pump, is to bathe tomorrow, & try Electricity on Tuesday; – he proposed the latter himself to Dr Fellowes, who made no objection to it, but I fancy we are all unanimous in expecting no advantage from it. At present I have no great notion of our staying here beyond the month.

But Edward was evidently advised to give the waters a longer trial, and nine days later Jane told Cassandra that she was 'not sorry, as it turns out, that our stay here has been lengthened'. She added:

> Edward has been pretty well for this last week, and as the waters have never *dis*agreed with him in any respect, we are

inclined to hope that he will derive advantage from them in the end. Everybody encourages us in this expectation, for they all say the effect of the waters cannot be negative, and many are the instances in which their benefit is felt afterwards more than on the spot.

But a week later she had to report:

Edward has not been well these last two days; his appetite has failed him, & he has complained of sick & uncomfortable feelings, which with other symptoms makes us think of the Gout – perhaps a fit of it might cure him, but I cannot wish it to begin at Bath . . . . Mrs Williams need not pride herself on her knowledge of Dr Mapleton's success here; – she knows no more than everybody else knows in Bath. – There is not a Physician in the place who writes so many Prescriptions as he does. – I cannot help wishing that Edward had not been tied to Dr Fellowes, for had he come disengaged, we should all have recommended Dr Mapleton; my Uncle and Aunt as earnestly as ourselves.

The Mapletons were another family whom the Austens visited socially. 'I do not see the Miss Mapletons often, but just as often as I like; we are always very glad to meet, & I do not wish to wear out our satisfaction', added Jane on this occasion. Dr Mapleton, and his daughters Jane, Marianne and Christiana, lived at 11 The Circus. Dr Mapleton's skills were not enough to save Marianne from a premature death, on 18 May 1801, at a time when Jane Austen was again in Bath. 'You will be sorry to hear that Marianne Mapleton's disorder has ended fatally', she wrote to Cassandra; 'she was believed out of danger on Sunday, but a sudden relapse carried her off the next day. – So affectionate a family must suffer severely; & many a girl on early death has been praised into an Angel I believe, on slighter pretensions to Beauty, Sense & Merit than Marianne.'

Despite being 'tied' to Dr Fellowes, Edward evidently consulted with other medical men, since later in the same letter of 19 June 1799 Jane wrote:

Edward has seen the Apothecary to whom Dr Millman recommended him, a sensible, intelligent Man, since I began this – & he attributes his present little feverish indisposition to his having ate something unsuited to his stomach. – I do not understand that Mr Anderton suspects the Gout at all; – The occasional particular glow in the hands and feet, which we considered as a symptom of that Disorder, he only calls the effect of the Water in promoting a better circulation of the blood.

Dr Millman was perhaps Edward's physician at home, since his name is not given in the Bath Guide for 1800. Mr Anderton is listed as an apothecary of 4 Queen Square. (An apothecary had no medical degree and was something like our modern pharmacist, though entitled to visit patients and prescribe.)

Another apothecary with whom Jane had dealings on more than one occasion was William Bowen, who shared a practice with a Mr Spry at 1 Argyle Street, on the Bathwick side of Pulteney Bridge. From here he attended Mrs Austen in a severe illness which attacked her during her residence at 4 Sydney Place. She recovered and wrote the following humorous yet touching verses:

> Says Death, 'I've been trying these three weeks and more
> To seize an old Madam here at Number Four.
> Yet I still try in vain, tho' she's turned of three score;
>   To what is my ill success owing?'

> 'I'll tell you, old Fellow, if you cannot guess,
> To what you're indebted for your ill success –
> To the prayers of my husband, whose love I possess,
> To the care of my daughters, whom Heaven will bless,
>   To the skill and attention of Bowen.'[10]

Mr Bowen also attended Mr Austen in his last illness at Green Park Buildings. Though he had saved Mrs Austen unassisted, he advised calling in a physician when Mr Austen's danger was perceived, as Jane described in a letter to her brother Frank:

> He was taken ill on Saturday morning, exactly in the same way as heretofore, an oppression in the head, with fever, violent tremulousness, & the greatest degree of Feebleness. The same remedy of Cupping, which had before been so successful, was immediately applied to – but without such happy effects. The attack was more violent, & at first he seemed scarcely at all relieved by the operation. – Towards the Evening however he got better, had a tolerable night, & yesterday morning was so greatly amended as to get up & join us at breakfast as usual, & walk about with only the help of a stick, & every symptom was then so favourable that when Bowen saw him at one, he felt sure of his doing

perfectly well. – But as the day advanced, all these comfortable appearances gradually changed; the fever grew stronger than ever, & when Bowen saw him at ten at night, he pronounc'd his situation to be most alarming. – At nine this morning he came again – & by his desire a Physician was called in; – Dr Gibbs – But it was then absolutely a lost case –. Dr Gibbs said that nothing but a Miracle could save him, and at about twenty minutes after Ten he drew his last gasp.

Dr Gibbes appears in the Bath Guide with an e in his name, and an address at 28 Gay Street.

Four months after Mr Austen's death one of his former pupils, William Buller, now Vicar of Colyton in Devon, arrived in Bath in quest of a cure. On 8 April 1805 Jane wrote:

We heard with much surprise that Mr Buller had called while we were out. He left his address, & I am just returned from seeing him & his wife in their Lodgings, 7 Bath Street. His errand as you may suppose is health. It had been often recommended to him to try Bath, but his coming now seems to have been chiefly in consequence of his sister Susan's wish that he would put himself under the care of Mr Bowen. – Having very lately heard from Colyton & that account so tolerable I was very much astonished – but Buller has been worse again since he wrote to me. – His Habit has always been billious, but I am afraid it must be too late for these waters to do him any good; for tho' he is altogether in a more comfortable state as to Spirits & appetite than when I saw him last, & seems equal to a good deal of quiet walking, his appearance has exactly that of a confirmed Decline.

Three days later she added a postscript to this letter, 'Buller has begun to take the Waters, so that it will soon appear whether they can do anything for him'. They could not; though perhaps like General Tilney he would not give them a fair trial, for, anxious about the children left at home, by 21 April the Bullers had left Bath as suddenly as they had arrived. He died in December of the following year, aged just 32.

The last Bath doctor to figure in Jane's correspondence was Dr Caleb Hillier Parry, of 27 The Circus. Some of the fees which this eminent man took off his rich patients were used in property speculation, for he was 'actively concerned', according to Walter Ison, in the development of Camden Crescent, Sir Walter Elliot's prestigious (and precarious!) address. Jane Austen's tone is rather cynical when she refers to this doctor in a series of letters beginning in September 1813. Edward's mother-in-law, Lady Bridges, travelled from her home in Kent, via Chawton where she stayed with Edward and his children in the Great House, to Bath for the sake of her health, staying at the White Hart Inn while lodgings were found. With her were her son Henry and his family; her unmarried daughter Louisa; and an orphaned grand-daughter Fanny Cage, who seems to have furnished some hints for Louisa Musgrove. Jane, who accompanied Edward back to his other home in Kent, wrote to Cassandra on 15 September:

> Now for Bath. Poor F. Cage has suffered a good deal from her accident. The noise of the White Hart was terrible to her. They will keep her quiet, I dare say. *She* is not so much delighted with the place as the rest of the party, probably, as she says herself, from having been less well, but she thinks she should like it better in season. The streets are very empty now, and the shops not so gay as she expected. They are at No. 1 Henrietta Street, the corner of Laura Place, and have no acquaintance at present but the Bramstons. Lady Bridges drinks at the Cross Bath, her son at the Hot, and Louisa is going to bathe. Dr Parry seems to be half starving Mr Bridges, for he is restricted to much such a diet as James's bread, water and meat, and is never to eat so much of that as he wishes, and he is to walk a great deal – walk till he drops, I believe – gout or no gout. It really is to that purpose. I have not exaggerated.

A month later she reported:

> Lady B continues very well & Dr Parry's opinion is that while the water agrees with her she ought to remain there . . . It will end perhaps in a fit of the Gout which may prevent her coming away. Louisa thinks her Mother's being so well may be quite as much owing to her being so much out of doors, as to the Water. Lady B is going to try the Hot Pump; the Cross Bath being about to be painted. Louisa is particularly well herself, & thinks the Water has been of use to her.

On 3 November Jane wrote:

> I shall now tell you something of the Bath party – & still a Bath party they are, for a fit of Gout came on last week. – The accounts of Lady B. are as good as can be under the circumstance, Dr P. says it appears a good sort of Gout and her spirits are better than usual, but as to her coming away, of course it is all uncertainty.

And three days later she told Cassandra:

My Brother has had a letter from Louisa today, of an unwelcome nature; – they are to spend the winter in Bath. It was just decided on. Dr Parry wished it – not from thinking the water necessary to Lady B – but that he might be better able to judge how far his treatment of her, which is totally different from anything she is used to – is right; & I suppose he will not mind having a few more of her Ladyship's guineas. His system is a lowering one. He took twelve ounces of Blood from her when the Gout appeared, & forbids wine etc. Hitherto the plan agrees with her. *She* is well satisfied to stay, but it is a sore disappointment to Louisa and Fanny. The H. Bridges leave them on Tuesday, & they mean to move into a smaller house.

Jane returned from Kent and nothing more is heard of Lady Bridges' health until March, when she was visited in Bath by Edward and his eldest daughter, Fanny. In anticipation of this visit, Fanny wrote to an ex-governess, Miss Chapman, that she was going to 'a still gayer part of the world' than Kent had proved that winter, and that as it was now 'just the Bath season' she expected to 'grow quite dissipated'. (In the event she attended just two balls, at the Upper and Lower Rooms respectively, where according to her diary she was 'much amused', but which she later told Miss Chapman had been 'very stupid' – an early touch, perhaps, of the hypocrisy which was to mark Fanny's character in old age.)[11] Fanny and her father stayed two weeks in Bath. On their way home they passed through London, where Jane was staying with her brother Henry. 'The accounts are not capital of Lady B.' Jane told Cassandra, and later in the same letter added, 'Edward heard from Louisa this morning. – Her mother does not get better, & Dr Parry talks of her beginning the Waters again; this will be keeping them longer in Bath.' In fact they returned to Kent that April.

The sick, the aged and the hypochondriac were therefore still an important part of Bath's economy, well into the 19th century. So much so, indeed, that a good deal of the back page of every issue of the *Bath Chronicle* in Jane Austen's time was taken up with advertisements for pills: Female Pills, Scotch Pills, Vegetable Pills, Patent Pills, Roman Pills and Cordial Balm among them. Indeed, Bath was to become increasingly the resort of invalids and dowagers as the century progressed, giving rise to the invention of the Bath Chair, and to the atmosphere of rigid, gloomy, and increasingly shabby respectability which came to characterize the city for more than a century, until after the Second World War. In 1851, for example, there were 3,980 widows to 1,086 widowers in the city; 10,767 spinsters (at least a quarter of them domestic servants) to 4,057 bachelors.

Jane saw the birth of this trend, and in *Mansfield Park* has Mrs Rushworth, on the occasion of her son's marriage, 'remove herself, with true dowager propriety, to Bath – there to parade over the wonders of Sotherton in the evening parties – enjoying them as thoroughly perhaps in the animation of a card table as she had ever done on the spot'. Or, as Sir Walter Elliot laments in *Persuasion:*

> The worst of Bath was, the number of its plain women. He did not mean to say that there were no pretty women, but the number of the plain was out of all proportion. He had frequently observed, as he walked, that one handsome face would be followed by thirty, or five and thirty frights; and once, as he had stood in a shop in Bond-street, he had counted eighty-seven women go by, one after another, without there being a tolerable face among them. It had been a frosty morning, to be sure, a sharp frost, which hardly one woman in a thousand could stand the test of. But still, there certainly were a dreadful multitude of ugly women in Bath; and as for the men! they were infinitely worse. Such scare-crows as the streets were full of!

Jane Austen, her mother and sister were, by their circumstances, well qualified to be part of this trend towards shabby, mainly female gentility, respectability and hypochondria. In the spring of 1806, at the age of only 30, Jane may well have looked ahead gloomily and helplessly to another 30 years of such a life, visualizing, with her extraordinary empathy for the spirit of her age, the continued decline in the vitality of Bath. It is no wonder, then, that she was to use the word 'escape', of her own release, in such a heartfelt way. The waters which had once made Bath the most fashionable resort in the kingdom, which had been the original source of all its gaiety and novelty, were increasingly attracting the old, the ill, the desperately genteel, and the woman without a man. Jane Austen saw much to criticize in the values of both sets of people: the frivolous and fashionable, and the dull, pathetic and narrow-minded. Bath furnished her not only with a gallery of individuals to observe and exercise her trenchant wit upon, but with ideas about society that give her novels much of their enduring fascination and depth.

Milsom Street

CHAPTER FOUR

Shopping

If many people came to Bath primarily to take the waters, the main or secondary purpose of many others was to shop for goods unobtainable at home. Supported by a constant influx of wealthy visitors, the Bath shops were second only to those in London in the variety and fashionableness of their merchandise; and being more closely grouped together, were more convenient for female shopping on foot. As Mrs Allen tells Henry Tilney:

> Bath is a charming place, sir; there are so many good shops
> here. – We are sadly off in the country . . . . Now here one
> can step out of doors and get a thing in five minutes.

Among those characters whose primary motive in coming to Bath is shopping are: Captain Harville, whose 'business' is to choose a frame for the miniature of Captain Benwick; and Henrietta Musgrove, who joins the party as 'it was thought a good opportunity for Henrietta to come and buy wedding-clothes for herself and her sister'. Even where shopping was not the chief objective of the visit, bringing one's own wardrobe up-to-date, carrying out commissions for friends left in the country, and choosing gifts to take back, occupied a large portion of time – at any rate of female time – in Bath.

But before such pleasurable shopping could be indulged in, there was the more basic need of laying in provisions for one's stay. Food vies with fashion in the shopping references of Jane Austen's letters from the city. It was less interesting, perhaps, but more essential. On the day after their arrival in Bath in May 1799 she told Cassandra:

> Edward seemed rather fagged last night, and not very brisk
> this morning; but I trust the bustle of sending for tea, coffee,
> and sugar etc., and going out to taste a cheese himself, will
> do him good.

Presumably the quality of these items was so variable, that landladies preferred each party of guests to choose them for themselves. Food was mostly bought at market. 'There was hardly any veal to be got at market this morning', complains Mrs Thorpe. The Bath Guide of 1800 boasts:

> The principal markets are kept on Wednesdays and Saturdays,
> & plentifully supplied with every kind of provisions, generally

at moderate prices. Fresh butter (equal to any in England) is brought in from the country every morning, and the butchers who live in the city supply the inhabitants with the best of meat every day of the week. The markets for fish are Mondays, Wednesdays and Fridays and are thought to excel those of any inland town in the kingdom.

Despite this claim, Jane found the butter bad one breakfast time in Queen Square (but the rolls at the same meal were good). Other dishes which the Austens enjoyed during this visit to Bath were gooseberry pie and gooseberry pudding. 'We are used to live very well', confessed Jane. Perhaps the landlady prepared these delicacies, or perhaps they were bought ready-made at a pastry-cook's like Mollands, the shop in Milsom Street where Anne Elliot shelters from the rain. In *Northanger Abbey*, too, Jane Austen writes of ladies crossing Cheap Street 'in quest of millinery or pastry'.

The price of food in the Bath markets took on a deeper significance for the Austens when they arrived in Bath to take up residence. In the country, almost every item the family consumed had been grown, reared, baked, brewed or churned at home. Supervising the farm and the dairy, gardening and cooking had taken up a great deal of both parents' time, Mrs Austen's especially. The move to Bath eased this burden, but the effect on the family budget, in any case reduced, and diminished too by house-rent, must have been something of an unknown quantity. Jane, who was to be insecure from this date until the end of her life about money matters, betrayed a keen interest in food prices in her very first letter to Cassandra. After mentioning that a cucumber cost one shilling – the same price as a whole pound of butter! – she returned to the subject:

> I am not without hopes of tempting Mrs Lloyd to settle in Bath; meat is only 8d per pound, butter 12d, and cheese 9½d. You must carefully conceal from her, however, the exorbitant price of fish: a salmon has been sold at 2s 9d per pound the whole fish. The Duchess of York's removal is expected to make that article more reasonable.

The glory of Bath, however, was not its food but its fashion. Provincial ladies, who had few means of knowing what were the latest trends, not only reported their observations eagerly to their friends back home by letter, or by word of mouth when they returned, but on arrival felt obliged to make certain alterations in their dress. Thus, when Mrs Allen and Catherine Morland arrive in Bath from the neighbouring county of Wiltshire, before they attend any of the public functions, they spend 'three or four days . . . in learning what was mostly worn, & buying clothes of the latest fashion'. Learning could be done by observation of the fashions in the streets, or by consulting the *Bath Journal*, which regularly gave updates under the headings 'Full dress', 'Morning dress' and 'Head dress'.

In May 1799 the chief fashion news concerned the trimming of hats. Jane reported to Cassandra:

> Flowers are very much worn, & Fruit is still more the thing. Eliz: has a bunch of strawberries, & I have seen Grapes, Cherries, Plumbs and Apricots – There are likewise Almonds & raisins, french plumbs & Tamarinds at the Grocers, but I have never seen any of them in hats. – A plumb or green-gage would cost three shillings; Cherries & grapes about 5 I believe – but this is at some of the dearest shops; – My aunt has told me of a very cheap one near Walcot church, to which I shall go in quest of something for you.

In a subsequent letter she wrote:

> We have been to the cheap shop, and very cheap we found it, but there are only flowers made there, no fruit; and as I could get four or five very pretty sprigs of the former for the same money which would procure only one Orleans plumb – in short, could get more for three or four shillings than I could have the means of bringing home – I cannot decide on the fruit till I hear from you again. Besides, I cannot help thinking that it is more natural to have flowers grow out of the head than fruit. What do you think on that subject?

Two years later, she was again in Bath without Cassandra, and hastened to keep her sister up to date with fashions:

> I find my straw bonnet looking very much like other people's, and quite as smart. Bonnets of cambric muslin on the plan of Lady Bridges' are a good deal worn, and some of them are very pretty; but I shall defer one of that sort till your arrival. Bath is getting so very empty that I am not afraid of doing too little. Black gauze cloaks are worn as much as anything.

A few days later she added: 'When you have made Martha's bonnet you must make her a cloak of the same sort of materials; they are very much worn here, in different forms – many of them just like her black silk spencer, with a trimming round the arm-holes instead of sleeves; some are long before, and some long all round like C[atherine] Bigg's'.

When their niece Fanny Knight paid a short visit to Bath in March 1814, Jane was able to pass on the news of clothes to Cassandra: 'Ribbon trimmings are all the fashion in Bath'. The newer styles of the city also made her wait for a new dress in 1801:

> I shall want two new coloured gowns for the summer, for my pink one will not do more than clear me from Steventon. I shall not trouble you, however, to get more than one of them, and that is to be a plain brown cambric muslin, for morning wear; the other, which is to be a very pretty yellow and white cloud, I mean to buy in Bath.

Mrs Leigh Perrot thought wearing white 'an absurd pretension in this place'. Eleanor Tilney, however, always wore white in Bath, and was elegance itself. Jane persisted in her desire for white, and having chosen a length of material, took it to a local dressmaker to make up. 'Mrs Musssell has got my gown', she reported on 5 May 1801, going on to give Cassandra an exact description of how the gown was to be made up. All such details had to be agreed between client and dressmaker, as there were no paper patterns to go by. The results were not always satisfac-tory; on 27 May Jane wrote to Cassandra, 'I will engage Mrs Mussell as you desire. She made my dark gown very well & may therefore be trusted I hope with yours – but she does not always succeed with light colours. My white one I was obliged to alter a good deal'. The Austen ladies may have taken their lengths of material – known, even before making up, as gowns – to the woman elected to make it up for them, or have been visited by her in their home. Mrs Croft, in the cancelled chapter of *Persuasion*, is closeted in her room with 'her mantua maker', a term left over from a mid-18th century style of dress.[12]

Other purchases were also made: 'My mother has ordered a new bonnet, and so have I; both white strip, trimmed with white ribbon'.

Friends and relatives left at home charged those lucky enough to go to Bath with commissions. As Jane wrote in jest,

> Martha & You were just in time with your commissions, for two o'clock Monday was the last hour of my receiving them; – the office is now closed.

She had previously written,

> I will lay out all the little Judgement I have in endeavouring
> to get such stockings for Anna as she will approve; – but I
> do not know that I shall execute Martha's commission at
> all, for I am not fond of ordering shoes, & at any rate they
> shall all have flat heels.

She continued the playful reluctance with:

> I am afraid I cannot undertake to carry Martha's shoes
> home, for tho' we had plenty of room in our Trunks when
> we came, we shall have many more things to take back, &
> I must allow besides for *my* packing.

That is, one of the Steventon servants had packed the trunks
for their journey to Bath, but there was no such help available
for the return journey. The inexperience of Catherine Morland
and Eleanor Tilney in packing their own clothes is commented
on in *Northanger Abbey*.

Among the 'many more things' to be taken back to Steventon
were cloaks for herself and Cassandra. First she bought her own:

> My cloak is come home and here follows the pattern of its
> lace. [Jane drew the design.] If you do not think it wide
> enough, I can give 3d a yard more for yours, & not go
> beyond the two guineas, for my cloak altogether does not
> cost quite two pounds.

A few days later, having received her sister's instructions, she
was able to write: 'I have got your cloak home, which is quite
delightful – as delightful at least as half the circumstances which
are called so'.

As well as making purchases for themselves, and on commission
for their relatives and friends, ladies visiting Bath had also to
think about buying presents to surprise those left at home. Before
her visit to Bath in 1799, Jane had evidently agreed with Cassandra
that she should bring back a gift for their sister-in-law Mary, to
be paid for by the sisters jointly. Jane duly reported:

> Now I shall give you the history of Mary's veil, in the
> purchase of which I have so considerably involved you that
> it is my duty to economise for you in the flowers. I had no
> difficulty in getting a muslin veil for half a guinea, and not
> much more in discovering afterwards that the muslin was
> thick, dirty and ragged, and therefore would by no means
> do for a united gift. I changed it consequently as soon as I
> could, and, considering what a state my imprudence had
> reduced me to, I thought myself lucky in getting a black
> lace one for sixteen shillings. I hope half that sum will not

greatly exceed what you had intended to offer upon the altar of sister-in-law affection.

The three principal shopping streets mentioned in the novels are Bond Street, Milsom Street and Bath Street. It is in a shop in Bond Street (presumably waiting for his daughter to make some purchase) that Sir Walter was standing when he counted the 87 plain women go by. And when Catherine Morland, 'having occasion for some indispensable yard of ribbon which must be bought without a moment's delay, walked out into the town', it was in Bond Street that she overtook 'the second Miss Thorpe, as she was loitering towards Edgar's Buildings between two of the sweetest girls in the world, who had been her dear friends all the morning'.

Earlier in the novel, Isabella Thorpe tells Catherine, 'I saw the prettiest hat you can imagine, in a shop window in Milsom Street just now – very like yours, only with coquelicot ribbons instead of green'. Milsom Street's being such a main thoroughfare between the upper and lower parts of the town made it highly conducive to window-shopping by the unlikeliest of people, as Anne Elliot finds on her way home one morning:

> In walking up Milsom-street, she had the good fortune to meet with the Admiral. He was standing by himself, at a printshop window, with his hands behind him, in earnest contemplation of some print.

'Here I am, you see, staring at a picture,' he tells her. 'I can never get by this shop without stopping.' A few pages later, Anne, Elizabeth, Mrs Clay and Mr Elliot are in Milsom Street when it begins to rain, and the ladies turn into Molland's, the pastry-cook's, for shelter. Anne is distracted by the sight of Captain Wentworth when she finds 'Mr Elliot (always obliging) just setting off for Union-street on a commission of Mrs Clay's'. Captain Wentworth has only just arrived in Bath, but has lost no time in doing some essential shopping. He tells Anne:

> 'I have equipped myself properly for Bath already, you see,' (pointing to a new umbrella).

Finally there is Bath Street, that very gracious new street, built in 1791, to connect the King's Bath and Pump Room with the Hot and Cross Baths. Jane Austen uses the location twice in her novels, and each time in connection with sly, designing characters. Isabella Thorpe, in a 'strain of shallow artifice' which can no longer impose on the maturing Catherine Morland, writes towards

Shop in Bond Street

the end of the novel of Frederick Tilney, whom she has lost: 'The last time we met was in Bath-street, and I turned directly into a shop that he might not speak to me; – I would not even look at him. He went into the Pump Room afterwards; but I would not have followed him for all the world'. And at the end of the other Bath novel, *Persuasion*, Bath Street also plays its part. Mary Musgrove, at the White Hart hotel, 'in her station at a window overlooking the entrance to the Pump Room', sees Mrs Clay and Mr Elliot together, 'standing under the colonnade' which partially encloses the Abbey Churchyard from the street. 'I saw them turn the corner from Bath-street,' Mary declares to her companions. This is the first hint of the 'double game' played by these two devious characters.

Jane Austen herself had indulged in window shopping here, as she told Cassandra in May 1799: 'I saw some gauzes in a shop in Bath Street yesterday at only 4s a yard, but they were not so good or so pretty as mine.' This may have been the very shop which, only a few months later, was to involve her aunt, the highly respectable Mrs Leigh Perrot, in an experience of nightmare proportions. Small as was Jane's love for her aunt, her innocence and endurance, and the whole horrific episode, may have prompted Jane Austen to connect Bath Street with the unprincipled characters of both *Northanger Abbey* and *Persuasion*.

The tale, truly 'stranger than fiction', has often been told, but no chapter on shopping in Bath in the world of Jane Austen could be complete without a brief recapitulation of this darker side to a pleasurable occupation. On 8 August 1799, less than two months after Jane left Bath following her holiday with Edward and his family, Mrs Leigh Perrot purchased some black lace at a shop in Bath Street kept by Miss Elizabeth Gregory. The shop assistant took the lace to the back of the shop to wrap it up, and included in the parcel a card of white lace, in a deliberate plan to blackmail the wealthy Leigh Perrots. Though it was obvious that the lace could not have been stolen, Mrs Leigh Perrot was arrested, and, refusing out of principle to buy herself off, endured imprisonment in Ilchester gaol until the Spring Assizes of the following March. The white lace was valued at 20 shillings, and the theft of any article above the value of one shilling was punishable by death or transportation. Mrs Austen offered the service of 'one, or both of her Daughters' to keep their aunt company through her long imprisonment, or to be present at the trial. Unselfishly, Mrs Leigh Perrot declined her offers. 'To have two Young Creatures gazed at in a public court would cut one to the very heart', she

The Colonnade

wrote. So Jane was spared this ordeal, and her aunt, though it was by no means a foregone conclusion, was acquitted after a trial lasting more than seven hours.

The episode did not, it seems, give any of the family a distaste for Bath (except perhaps Jane herself). The Leigh Perrots continued to reside there for at least half of every year, and it was only six months after the trial that Mr and Mrs Austen made their momentous decision to live permanently in Bath. All Jane could do to mark her outrage (and perhaps she did it unconsciously) was to give Bath Street dubious connections in the two novels she wrote about Bath.

CHAPTER FIVE

Walks and Drives

For Jane Austen, and for all her admirable characters, walking was one of the pleasures of life. The exercise, the enjoyment of being out in the open air, and the observation of landscape and the seasons, all made it a favourite pastime; and nowhere more so than in Bath, where it offered relief from crowds, confinement and mindless socializing. It is noticeable that in *Northanger Abbey* walks and drives play a large part in the heroine's life, which is mainly a happy one; whereas the more sombre tone of *Persuasion* is reinforced by a sense of physical constriction. Though the Bath passages of the novels take place at the same time of year – January and February – Anne takes no country walks or drives comparable with Catherine's.

There are very many beautiful walks around Bath, which is, like Rome, a town built on seven hills, and hence affords a variety of constantly changing prospects for walkers young and strong enough to tackle the steep slopes. Though no scenery was capable of rivalling that of her native Hampshire in her affections, Jane Austen was certainly appreciative of the countryside about Bath. 'We took a very charming walk from 6 to 8 up Beacon Hill, & across some fields to the Village of Charlcombe, which is sweetly situated in a little green Valley, as a village with such a name ought to be', Jane wrote of the evening of 31 May 1799. At this stage in their lives, Cassandra was evidently not familiar with Charlcombe, but like Eleanor Tilney both sisters took every opportunity to improve their knowledge. Of Catherine Morland, Jane writes:

> She had never taken a country walk since her arrival in Bath. Miss Tilney, to whom all the commonly-frequented environs were familiar, spoke of them in terms which made her all eagerness to know them too.

The walk which results from this conversation is the famous one to Beechen Cliff, 'that noble hill, whose beautiful verdure and hanging coppice render it so striking an object from almost every opening in Bath'. Beechen Cliff rises sharply immediately to the south of the river Avon, and to reach it Catherine and the Tilneys first follow the course of the river from Pulteney Bridge to the foot of Lyncombe Hill, a walk which reminds Catherine of the South of France, as described in her favourite 'horrid' novels. Under Henry Tilney's tutelage, 'when they gained the top of Beechen Cliff, she voluntarily rejected the whole city of Bath, as unworthy to make part of a landscape'. Few walkers who make the climb today could dismiss the breathtaking view quite so easily!

Another favourite walk with Jane was to Weston, a village about two miles west of Bath. 'We walked to Weston one evening last week, and liked it very much', Jane wrote in June 1799. 'Liked what very much? Weston? No, *walking* to Weston. I have not expressed myself properly, but I hope you will understand me'. Almost exactly two years later, the same walk was performed again, in company with a Mrs Chamberlayne, and Jane made an amusing story of it:

> Our grand walk to Weston was again fixed for yesterday, & was accomplished in a very striking manner; every one of the party declined it under some pretence or other except our two selves, & we had therefore a *tête à tête*, but *that* we should equally have had after the first two yards, had half the inhabitants of Bath set off with us. It would have amused you to see our progress; – we went up by Sion Hill, & returned across the fields; – in climbing a hill Mrs Chamberlayne is very capital; I could with difficulty keep pace with her – yet would not flinch for the world. – On plain ground I was quite her equal – and so we posted away under a hot sun, *she* without any parasol or shade to her hat, stopping for nothing & crossing the church yard at Weston with as much expedition as if we were afraid of being buried alive.

The following week the same two companions walked in the valleys of Lyncombe and Widcombe which lie immediately to the south of Bath. The manor house and church of Widcombe make this one of the prettiest walks from the city even today, when the tranquillity of their setting seems hardly altered. 'I walked yesterday morning with Mrs Chamberlayne to Lyncombe and Widcombe', Jane wrote on 26 May 1801. 'Mrs Chamberlayne's pace was not quite so magnificent on this second trial as in the first; it was nothing more than I could keep up with, without effort; and for many, many yards together on a raised narrow footpath I led the way. The walk was very beautiful as my companion agreed, whenever I made the observation.'

On another occasion, 'Miss Irvine spent yesterday evening with us, & we had a very pleasant walk to Twerton'. This was a village south west of Bath, on the more southerly of the two roads to Bristol, and the walk there would be a comparatively level one.

Weston Churchyard

Two other walks in or around Bath mentioned by Jane Austen are interesting because they remind us that she belonged to the great age of canal building. On 5 May 1801 she told Cassandra, 'Last night we walked by the Canal'. This must refer to the Kennet and Avon Canal, which branches from the River Avon at the south-east corner of Bath, and cuts through Sydney Gardens, very close to the Austens' home at Sydney Place, on its way to join the River Kennet in Berkshire. The Kennet and Avon Canal was constructed between 1796 and 1810; a map of 1800 shows that it had not yet reached Sydney Gardens, but by 1804 it is being shown, so presumably Jane observed this stage of its construction during her residence in Sydney Place. The 1801 walk may have been slightly southward of this, at Widcombe, where there is a flight of 6 locks, and perhaps was undertaken because her uncle, James Leigh Perrot, was deeply interested in feats of civil engineering. For just one week later, Jane wrote to Cassandra, 'My uncle . . . . and I are soon to take the long-plann'd walk to the Cassoon'. This has been identified as the 'caisson' or lift with a vertical rise of 46 feet at Combe Hay on the Somerset Coal Canal.[13] Built in 1798, the huge lock had been abandoned by the time of Jane Austen's visit in favour of an inclined plane, which in turn proved unsatisfactory, and by 1805 a flight of twenty-two locks was substituted. Jane Austen has been criticised for making few references to the effects of the Industrial Revolution upon the English countryside and economy during her lifetime; it is interesting that twice when she does mention technological innovations, they should be connected with Bath.

In speaking of a proposed walk to 'the Cassoon', the possibility exists that Jane was making a gentle joke at her uncle's expense, not only because she did not subsequently describe the walk as having taken place, but because the village of Combe Hay is three very hilly miles from Bath. Such a walk must have been beyond the gouty Mr Leigh Perrot's strength, if not her own: 'My uncle has quite got the better of his lameness, or at least his walking with a stick is the only remains of it,' runs the sentence immediately preceding reference to 'the long-plann'd walk'. I do not think that Jane, who once referred to herself and her friend Martha Lloyd as 'desperate walkers', would have blenched at the walk to Combe Hay on her own account. 'Yesterday was a busy day with me, or at least with my feet and stockings,' she wrote four years later, on 21 April 1805. 'I was walking almost all day long; I went to Sydney Gardens soon after one, and did not return till four, & after dinner I walked to Weston.' Her stamina, at

The Canal in Sydney Gardens

nearly 30 years old, was considerable, and evidently impressed young ladies who were not accustomed to venturing so far. The same month she wrote:

> I have walked with my Mother to St James' Square & Paragon; neither family at home. I have also been with the Cookes trying to fix Mary for a walk this afternoon, but as she was on the point of taking a *long* walk with some other lady, there is little chance of her joining us. I should like to know how far they are going; she invited me to go with them & when I excused myself as rather tired & mentioned my coming from St James' Square, she said 'that is a long walk indeed'.

Social walking of a less energetic kind was performed, especially on Sundays, in the city itself, the most fashionable location being 'the Crescent fields', the green slopes in front of the Royal Crescent which were 'never to be built on' according to contemporary maps. Jane Austen makes many references to this custom in both her letters and novels. It is in *Northanger Abbey* that she is most explicit. 'A fine Sunday in Bath empties every house of its inhabitants, and all the world appears on such an occasion to walk about and tell their acquaintance what a charming day it is.'

> As soon as divine service was over, the Thorpes and Allens eagerly joined each other; and after staying long enough in the Pump-room to discover that the crowd was insupportable, and that there was not a genteel face to be seen, which every body discovers every Sunday throughout the season, they hastened away to the Crescent, to breathe the fresh air of better company.

'On Sunday we went to church twice, & after evening service walked a little in the Crescent fields, but found it too cold to stay long', Jane told Cassandra in May 1801. Of another Sunday she wrote more cryptically: 'we did not walk long in the Crescent yesterday, it was hot & not crowded enough, so we went into the field'.

(Incidentally, it is not known where the Austens worshipped while they were in Bath; whether at the Abbey, one of the fine parish churches, or one of the many proprietary chapels which were built to accommodate the fashionable visitors. There is one reference in Jane's letters to 'our chapel'. This is most likely Laura Chapel, on the Bathwick estate, and would have been convenient for the Austens during their Sydney Place years. Built from funds raised on the tontine principle, and opened in

Weston Church

November 1795, it seated a congregation of 1,000 and was oval in shape. The Bath Guide says 'It is a very neat commodious building, and is rendered warm and comfortable in the winter season by fires in its recesses'. It was certainly Laura Chapel that Jane's niece Fanny attended during her visit to Bath in 1814. Unfortunately it was demolished this century, and only the entrance to it under an archway in Henrietta Street can now be seen.)

The identification of Sunday with walking in the Crescent was so complete that Jane Austen could write of 'the afternoon's Crescent of this day', when setting out to describe 'the pangs of Sunday' in *Northanger Abbey*. These pangs consist of the Thorpes' attempts to make Catherine defer her engagement to walk with the Tilneys, culminating in John Thorpe's intervention with the Tilneys themselves. Outraged, Catherine hurries after the Tilneys, to put the matter right. The point worth making is that Catherine walks 'as fast as the crowd would permit her' and 'quickening her pace when she got clear of the Crescent, she almost ran over the remaining ground till she gained the top of Milsom-street'. The crowds must indeed have been considerable.

It was not only on Sundays, however, that people might reasonably hope to meet their friends promenading on the broad pavement of the Crescent. When Catherine is engaged in other adventures, Mrs Allen and Mrs Thorpe, meeting in the Pump Room, 'agreed to take a turn in the Crescent', and there encountered Mrs Hughes, and the young Tilneys, with whom they 'walked along the Crescent together for half an hour'.

There is no mention in *Persuasion* of Sunday walking in the Crescent, or of that kind of public, social walking at all. Anne never walks out for pleasure, but that could be because she has no companion. Her two friends in Bath are Mrs Smith, who is disabled, and Lady Russell, who goes everywhere by carriage. 'Lady Russell took Anne out in her carriage almost every morning.' Although it is not specifically mentioned, it seems certain that Anne is with Lady Russell in the carriage when 'in returning down Pulteney-street she distinguished [Captain Wentworth] on the right hand pavement', since at one point Lady Russell 'drew back her head'.

As it is a 'toilsome walk' for Anne to get back home to Camden Place, this being taken about is perhaps highly convenient, and very kindly meant; but in consequence Anne rarely enjoys the air and exercise of a long walk that so delight her in the country. Neither on foot nor even in Lady Russell's carriage does she have the opportunity to escape, even for an hour, from the city. Hence this novel's powerful sense of confinement and constriction.

However, three walks of Anne's through the city itself are given in some detail. One morning it suits her to be dropped in the lower part of the town, presumably because she has some shopping to do, and meeting Admiral Croft in Milsom Street, she is escorted by him to Camden Place. He tells her that he has something to communicate, but at first talks of other things. 'She had hoped, when clear of Milsom-street, to have her curiosity gratified; but she was still obliged to wait, for the Admiral had made up his mind not to begin, till they had gained the greater space and quiet of Belmont.' This is a steep stretch of the road to Lansdown, and it is perhaps surprising that the Admiral can climb it and talk at the same time, but 'as soon as they were fairly ascending Belmont, he began'.

Anne's second walk is taken after she has begun to believe in the revival of Captain Wentworth's love. She walks down through the town, from her home to the inferior lodgings of her friend Mrs Smith. The state of the streets, especially in the lower part of the town, where many of the premises were devoted to all kinds of noxious trades, and where the poorer part of the population lived in overcrowded, unsanitary conditions, here impinges upon the otherwise elegant world of Regency Bath. As a resident of a nearby street had written to the Corporation in 1786, 'I am sorry that present circumstances makes your attention necessary in Avon Street, which with the large quantities of all kinds of nastiness thrown out by its inhabitants for a whole week together and the interspersion of here and there a group of pigs makes a perfect dung muckson from one end to the other'.[14] Conditions did not improve in the early part of the next century, and the area suffered a cholera epidemic in 1831. This was the seamy, forgotten side of Bath, of which Jane Austen was certainly aware:

> Prettier musings of high-wrought love and eternal constancy, could never have passed along the streets of Bath, than Anne was sporting with from Camden-place to Westgate-buildings. It was almost enough to spread purification and perfume all the way.

And finally there is that last, rapturous walk, as, their engagement renewed, Anne and Frederick 'slowly paced the gradual ascent' from Union Street, where, appropriately they are united, to 'the comparatively quiet and retired gravel walk'. The Gravel Walk was designed by the younger Wood to link his father's masterpiece, Queen Square, with his own, the Royal Crescent. Running

Gravel Walk

along behind the back gardens of one segment of the Circus and of Brock Street, it provides a traffic-free walk that is reasonably dry underfoot.

The two owners of carriages in *Persuasion*, Lady Russell and Lady Dalrymple, are too staid to suggest driving about the country as a way of passing the time. This is a complete contrast to

Northanger Abbey, where the vehicles are owned – or hired – by irresponsible young men, John Thorpe and James Morland. (The male sex seems generally on the move in the Bath of this novel; Catherine looks in vain for Henry Tilney 'among the walkers, the horsemen or the curricle-drivers of the morning' and on one occasion Eleanor reports that Henry 'has rid out this morning with my father'.) Catherine allows herself to be driven by John Thorpe twice, before learning from Mr Allen that 'Young men and women driving about the country in open carriages' is 'not quite the thing'. Although John Thorpe first promises to drive Catherine 'up Landsdown Hill' it is in fact to Claverton Down that he takes her. They are out from half-past twelve to past three o'clock. Though already learning to distrust and dislike Thorpe himself, Catherine 'gave herself up to all the enjoyment of air and exercise of the most invigorating kind, in a fine mild day of February'. The *Bath Guide* for 1800 lists both Lansdown and Claverton Down among the recommended drives:

> The publick roads about Bath have been much improved within these few years, and the access to the hills, Claverton and Lansdown (which was formerly very difficult) is now rendered safe, easy and pleasant, either on horseback or in carriages. The air that you breathe in on these hills is very beneficial to invalids, who ride to restore their health.
>
> Lansdown is one of the most conspicuous and happily situated hills in the west of England, and famous for the number of sheep fattened by its herbage . . . From hence you have a fine view of the Bristol Channel, city of Bristol, part of Wales, and a great part of Gloucestershire, Worcestershire and Wiltshire; and there is one point of view where the cities of Bath and Bristol may be seen at the same time.
>
> Claverton Down is also a very pleasant and agreeable airing for invalids, by whom it is much frequented . . . . To the right, as you descend this Down, is a seat that belonged to the late Ralph Allen esq . . . called Prior Park, which commands a most beautiful and picturesque prospect of the vale beneath and the surrounding hills, the city of Bath being the chief object.

Jane Austen herself was driven to yet another of the seven hills or downs which surround Bath. Her 'gentleman coachman' was a Mr Evelyn, a middle-aged friend of her brother Edward. 'There is now something like an engagement between us and the Phaeton, which to confess my frailty I have a great desire to go out in', she wrote to Cassandra on 26 May 1801. The following day she reported, 'I am just returned from my airing in the very bewitching Phaeton & four, for which I was prepared by a note from Mr E. soon after breakfast. We went to the top of Kingsdown and had a very pleasant drive.'

Catherine Morland's second experience of driving out with John Thorpe is less pleasant than the first, since he tricks her into breaking her engagement to walk with the Tilneys, and tempts her with lies about their own destination. The Tilneys, he says, have driven out in a phaeton up Lansdown Road; but when Catherine, having passed down Pulteney Street and through Laura Place, enters Argyle Buildings, she sees the Tilneys walking towards her own lodgings. Thorpe, refusing her pleas to stop, whisks her into the Market Place, and thence out on the Bristol Road. They get only to Keynsham, a village half way between Bristol and Bath, before having to turn back because of lack of time and daylight.

What tempts Catherine to go with Thorpe in the first place, and afterwards consoles her for the loss of her walk, is the promise of seeing Blaise Castle. 'The finest place in England – worth going fifty miles at any time to see', John Thorpe assures her.

'What, is it really a castle, an old castle?'
'The oldest in the kingdom.'
'But is it like what one reads of?'
'Exactly – the very same.'
'But now really – are there towers an long galleries?'
'By dozens.'

Anybody less näive than Catherine would have known that Blaise Castle was in fact scarcely 30 years old, an 18th century garden folly built by a wealthy sugar merchant, Thomas Farr, to adorn the grounds of his estate just outside Bristol. The joke, between Jane Austen and her contemporary readers, is on Catherine, but the censure is reserved for John Thorpe. Both his blatant dishonesty, and the poverty of his imagination – he can only echo Catherine's ideas, in comparison to Henry Tilney, who can keep her entertained with supposed doings at Northanger for mile after mile of a journey later in the book – are shown up by this conversation. Thus Jane Austen cleverly uses a landmark outside Bath for her artistic purposes, without actually conveying her characters there. And when the Thorpes and James Morland make a second attempt to reach Blaise, this time getting as far as Clifton, Jane Austen uses the occasion to effect the engagement between Isabella and James offstage. It is not necessary for either her readers, or her heroine, to go with them.

CHAPTER SIX

Public Entertainments

Ever since 'Beau' Nash had taken over as Master of Ceremonies at Bath, and had carried out his self-appointed task of regulating public conduct and of forcing everybody – from haughty duchess to coarse country squire – to conform to a standard of good manners and good breeding, the programme of evening entertainments and the rigid rules pertaining to them had been a most distinctive feature of Bath life. Nash died in 1762, but the influence of his character and his arrangements was still being felt half a century later. It is true that by the time Jane Austen came to reside in Bath, and certainly by the time she wrote *Persuasion*, there was a growing feeling in favour of private parties, as more exclusive and therefore more elegant than public assemblies. But that *Northanger Abbey* is an accurate depiction of Bath in the 1790s, and no mere nostalgic portrait of a vanished age, is proved by reference to the 1800 *Bath Guide*, with its descriptions of an elaborate programme of amusements which had hardly changed for 50 years.

From Monday to Saturday, not an evening need be unoccupied or unproductive of social contact. 'There are two dress balls every week, viz. Monday at the New Rooms and Friday at the Lower Rooms. Subscription one guinea to each room for which each subscriber has three tickets. There are also two Fancy Balls every week, viz. at the Lower Rooms on Tuesday, and at the New Rooms on Thursday; subscription half a guinea.' Left over from Nash's old autocratic rule was the instruction that the dancing was to 'begin as soon as possible after six o'clock, and finish *precisely* at eleven, even in the middle of a dance'. The list of attractions continues with 'Nine subscription concerts, and three choral nights, in the winter at the New Rooms, on Wednesday, under the direction of Mr Rauzzini. At the theatre the days of performances are in general, Tuesdays, Thursdays and Saturdays.'

Dancing, listening to music and going to the theatre were therefore the main occupations of the evening, with the addition of card-playing for non-dancing men like Mr Allen, available in an ante-room adjoining the main ballroom (though gaming had been illegal in Bath since 1745). Altogether it was a programme which maximized visitors' opportunities both to mix freely with one another, and to fill their leisure hours in novel ways – two of the chief motivations in coming to Bath. Neither music nor drama, of course, was easily obtainable in the country; certainly not to professional standards.

Such a highly organized programme of public gatherings, with everybody going to the same place on the same night, was of the utmost utility to Catherine Morland (and to the plot of *Northanger Abbey*), for without it she would have had no chance of working herself first into the consciousness, and then into the affections, of a total stranger, Henry Tilney. At the very beginning of their acquaintance, he interrogates her thus:

> 'Have you yet honoured the Upper Rooms?'
> 'Yes, sir, I was there last Monday.'
> 'Have you been to the theatre?'
> 'Yes, sir, I was at the play on Tuesday.'
> 'To the concert?'
> 'Yes, sir on Wednesday.'
> 'And are you altogether pleased with Bath?'
> 'Yes – I like it very well.'
> 'Now I must give one smirk, and then we may be rational again.'

Catherine's answers reveal that Henry knew exactly in what order to ask his questions! In fact two separate weeks of Catherine's life in Bath are given in daily detail, and if we follow her movements, filling in background information as we go, we will obtain not only a sound understanding of organized social life in Bath, but an appreciation of Jane Austen's skill in weaving her story around it.

Catherine arrives, perhaps, on a Thursday or Friday, since on the following Friday she tells Henry Tilney that she has been in Bath 'about a week'. A few days are taken up in 'learning what was mostly worn' before she can appear in public. Her first such appearance is on Monday, at the Upper Rooms, when she is incommoded by the crowd, yet, knowing nobody, receives no requests to dance. The following two evenings, as she informs Henry, are occupied by the play and the concert. On Thursday evening perhaps she stays quietly at home. Then comes the memorable Friday when she first goes to the Lower Rooms and is introduced by its master of ceremonies, James King, to Henry Tilney.

'There are two sets of Assembly-Rooms in this city', the Guide informed intending visitors. The Lower Rooms, dating from as early as 1708, with additions in 1720 and 1749, were well situated at the time they were built, being in the most public part of the old town, near the bowling green, John Wood's Parades, and the various walks laid out by the river. 'The view of the river, valley and adjacent hills, makes this one of the pleasantest morning rooms in the kingdom', the Guide continues. 'There is a publick breakfast or agreeable morning promenade every Wednesday, at the Lower Rooms, during the season.' Jane Austen makes no mention of this daytime use of the Lower Rooms, which are often found in memoirs of the period referred to as Simpson's Rooms, after their original owner. Mr King was the Master of Ceremonies here during the 1790s, but by 1806 had been succeeded by Mr Le Bas, who is mentioned in a letter from Mrs Austen of April of that year: 'Mr Le Bas's ball on Fryday [sic] at the lower rooms will probably be but a thin one'.

However, as the fashionable centre of gravity was drawn by the expansion of the town up the northern slopes, these rooms were found inconvenient by many visitors. It was customary to go home from evening assemblies by chair – a covered seat on poles carried by two men. At the end of her first ball Catherine 'went to her chair in good humour with everybody', and on another occasion, 'her spirits danced within her, as she danced in her chair all the way home'. Even so, a long haul up the town must have been an uncomfortable, even a mildly terrifying, way to end the day. The New or Upper Rooms were built in 1769-71 to satisfy the needs of residents in the newly laid-out upper parts of the town, and they occupied a site betwen the Circus and the portion of the Lansdown Road known as Belmont. Not surprisingly, there was considerable rivalry between the two sets of rooms; yet by offering attractions on alternate evenings, both managed to keep in business well into the 19th century, when the Lower Rooms eventually fell into disuse.

Of course, families who lived within comfortable distance of either set of rooms could and did patronize both. That was the case with the Allens, Thorpes and Tilneys. Jane Austen seems to have preferred the Upper Rooms, which is not surprising, since they were more modern and spacious. Only one description of a Bath assembly survives in her letters. On 12 May 1801 she wrote:

> In the evening I hope you honoured my Toilette and Ball with a thought; I dressed myself as well as I could, & had all my finery much admired at home. By nine o'clock my Uncle, Aunt & I entered the rooms & linked Miss Winstone on to us. Before tea it was a rather dull affair; but then before tea did not last long, for there was only one dance, danced by four couple. Think of four couple, surrounded

by about an hundred people, dancing in the Upper Rooms at Bath! After tea we *cheered up*; the breaking up of private parties sent some scores more to the Ball & tho' it was still shockingly & inhumanly thin for this place, there were people enough I suppose to have made five or six very pretty Basingstoke assemblies.

The shortage of people was because the season was coming to a close. Jane added that they may go to the rooms again next Monday, 'which is to be really the last time'. Five years but one month later, in April 1806, we hear of her again at the Upper Rooms, when her mother writes that the 'ball on Monday was not a very *full* one, not more than a *thousand*'.

The morning after meeting Henry Tilney in the Lower Rooms, Catherine Morland hastens away to look for him in the Pump Room, but is disappointed for he has in fact left Bath temporarily. Instead she begins her acquaintance with Isabella Thorpe, whom she sees again that night at the theatre. On Sunday the Thorpes and Allens worship at the same chapel, and meet afterwards to walk in the Crescent.

The next 'eight or nine days' are skipped over as Catherine develops her friendship with Isabella, spends her time reading novels, and wonders whether she will ever seen Henry Tilney again. Catherine and Isabella are not actually described as visiting a lending library, yet presumably their voracious appetites for 'horrid novels' could only be satisfied by doing so. In the last decade of the century there were nine flourishing private lending libraries in the city, and they could be said to form part of the 'public entertainment' of the place. A piece of anonymous doggerel written in 1811 gives the best idea of what they were like, and it is very easy to imagine Catherine and Isabella among their customers. The Austens too were surely subscribers, having sold all their own books on leaving Steventon, and being, as Jane wrote once, 'novel-readers and not ashamed of being so'.

> To the left of the door there's a fireplace and there
> You may lounge, if you please, on a bench or a chair.
> A little way on to the right you'll behold
> The books that are bound up in calf and in gold;
> Not far, on a table, neglectfully lie
> The volumes that nobody chooses to buy;
> There's an essay on sepulchres – Emily – Hector –
> What a pity that hero should want a protector!
> In yonder recess you see novels, romances,
> Wise, witty and horrid, made up to all fancies.[15]

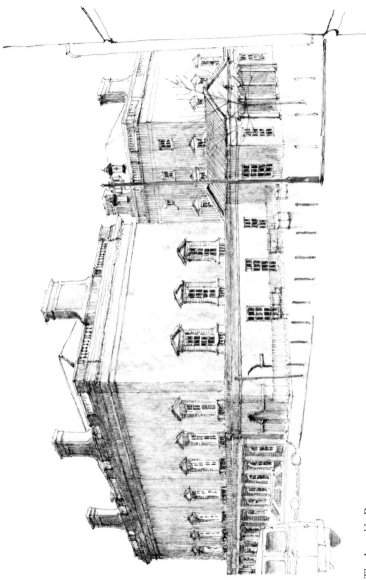

The Assembly Rooms

(New books advertised in the *Bath Journal* in May 1801, the month that Jane came to live in Bath, included such amusing titles as *Castle of St Donats, Fugitive of the Forest, The Nocturnal Visit, Children of the Abbey, Monk of the Grotto* and *Emily of Lucerne!*)

The chronology of *Northanger Abbey* becomes specific again on a Monday, a fortnight from Catherine's first appearance at the Upper Rooms. During the course of the morning James Morland and John Thorpe arrive unexpectedly in Bath, the latter immediately engaging Catherine to dance with him at the Upper Rooms that night. The two families agree to unite in the Octagon Room, the elegant ante-chamber which nearly 20 years later is to witness the meeting, charged with suppressed emotion, between Anne Elliot and Captain Wentworth, as they wait to go into the concert room. In this room, on Mondays functioning as a ballroom, Mr Tilney reappears, in company with his sister. Introducing three new characters in one day and re-introducing her hero, Jane Austen has now assembled all the cast for a week of complication and misunderstanding constructed around the Bath calendar.

On Tuesday Catherine is driven by John Thorpe up to Claverton Down, and in the evening the Allens, Thorpes and Morlands all meet at the theatre. On Wednesday morning Catherine encounters Eleanor Tilney at the Pump Room, and enquires, 'Shall you be at the cotillion ball tomorrow?' There is a slight change of fashion to be noted here between 1790 and 1800. What the 1800 Guide calls a 'Fancy Ball' was called a 'Cotillion Ball' in 1790; and when Catherine arrives at the Upper Rooms (Wednesday having been passed over without comment), she has to wait until 'the cotillions were over, and the country dancing begun' before she sees the Tilneys. Now her happiness is complete, for she is not only asked to dance by Henry, but invited on a country walk the following morning by his sister. Instead of fulfilling this engagement, she is tricked into driving out again by John Thorpe, and obliged to spend that evening, Friday, at the Thorpes' lodgings, while Isabella repeatedly expresses her satisfaction at not being at the Lower Rooms, and her pity for those who are.

On Saturday morning Catherine attempts to call on the Tilneys to make her explanation and apology, but she is not admitted. 'Dejected and humbled, she had even some thoughts of not going with the others to the theatre that night; but it must be confessed that they were not of long continuance: for she soon recollected, in the first place, that she was without any excuse for staying at home; and in the second, that it was a play she wanted very much to see.' Henry Tilney arrives between the fourth and fifth acts of the comedy; since two plays (usually completely incongruous) were always performed each evening, it is presumably the following piece that he has come to see. In the interval Catherine convinces him of her innocence, and though her trials are by no means over, public occasions now recede from the scene. Nevertheless, 'Monday, Tuesday, Wednesday, Thursday, Friday and Saturday have now passed before the reader', who can only marvel at the art which has made a fixed set of events conduce to the development and revelation of character.

The theatre which Catherine attended without fail every Tuesday and Saturday was the old theatre, at Orchard Street near the Abbey. The street itself had been built after the dissolution of the monasteries on orchard ground belonging to the Prior of Bath, and the theatre dated from 1750, though it was modernized several times in the next 50 years. The auditorium was perfectly rectangular, and lined with boxes, in which were the only seats bookable in advance (hence the term 'box office'), at a cost of 3s per seat. This theatre was granted a royal patent in 1768, and was the first provincial playhouse entitled to call itself 'Theatre Royal'. Ten years later the theatre in Bristol was similarly dignified, and for many years the two theatres, only 13 miles apart, were under the same management. This explains why plays were presented in Bath only on Tuesdays, Thursdays and Saturdays, for on alternate weekdays the same company, with the same props, were playing in the neighbouring city. It must have been an exhausting routine, especially as a different pair of plays was performed on each night of the week.[16]

There is certainty of Jane Austen's visiting the Orchard Street theatre only once, though it is inconceivable that she should not have seen many plays during her five winters' residence in the city. Indeed, it has been calculated that, with the system of repertoire then in operation, she had no fewer than six separate opportunities between 1801 and 1806 to see a performance of *Lovers Vows*, the play so integral to the plot of *Mansfield Park*.[17] The play on Saturday 22 June 1799 which she saw was Charles Dibden's *The Birthday* – with *Bluebeard* as afterpiece!

By the time of Jane Austen's residence in Bath, both the small size and the cramped and inconvenient location of the Orchard Street theatre were causing grumbles of discontent in the local press. From 1802 various sites for a splendid new theatre were being discussed, and in August 1804 the decision was made to build between Beaufort Square, Sawclose and St John's Court:

still within the area of the old town, but on its north west corner, and immediately adjacent to Chandos Buildings. Money was raised on the tontine principal (as it was for the building of many of the private chapels in Bath) and work proceeded so satisfactorily that the new theatre was complete with its elaborate decoration, and fully ready for occupation, less than a year after the first stone was laid. The last performance at the Orchard Street theatre was given on 13 July 1805: Otway's *Venice Preserved*. When the new winter season began, theatregoers had to get used to the new location. The new house opened on 12 October 1805 with a performance of Shakespeare's *Richard III* ('to which will be added the musical farce of the *Poor Soldier*', promised the playbill).

Seats in the boxes were now 5s, in the Pit 3s, and in the Gallery 1s 6d. The auditorium was 120 feet in length, 60 feet in breadth, and 70 feet in height. There were three tiers of boxes, and the decor was predominantly crimson and gold. As well as better accommodation for the audience, and much better facilities backstage, the advantages of the new threatre included its having three separate entrances, which prevented the dreadful crush on arriving and leaving which had been one of the principal complaints against the Orchard Street house.

It was in this more elegant building, therefore, that Charles Musgrove secured a box, to seat nine, for a Saturday evening performance, and was persuaded by his mother to change it for one the following Tuesday. By Tuesday, Anne and Captain Wentworth were reunited in understanding, and we may suppose that the chatter of the other seven left them with moments enough for private conversation, in the intervals of the play.

Again, it would seem inconceivable that Jane Austen did not visit the new theatre at least once during its first season, which coincided with her final winter in Bath. Following the death of Mr Austen in January 1805, the family finances were tight that year, but this may not have been the only reason why she and Cassandra did not accompany their friend Martha to *Macbeth*. On Thursday 10 April 1806, Mrs Austen wrote to her daughter-in-law (and Martha Lloyd's sister) Mary:

> Anna is quite well, Cassandra and Martha a good deal better; the latter ventured to the Play on Tuesday evening, it was an exertion, but an engagement of long standing & an earnest desire to see and hear Cooke in the character of Macbeth encouraged her to venture. Jane called on her yesterday and found her pretty well, only a little headache, nervous I suppose from the fatigue. The particulars of her accident,

The Old Theatre Royal

I conclude, you have had from Mrs Craven . . . Cooke, I dare say, will have as full houses tonight & Saturday, as he had on Tuesday.

George Frederick Cooke was a fine Shakespearean actor, and, along with Sarah Siddons (whose fame was founded in the Orchard Street theatre) and her brother John Philip Kemble, was among the notable thespians who regularly played in Bath, visiting both the old and new theatres. But there was a curious tradition attaching to the performance of *Macbeth* in Bath, which, it has been suggested, must have marred it for the discriminating. When Kemble took the part in 1802, the witches made a great deal of their parts by performing a ludicrous dance, which 'brought the house down'. Kemble requested its discontinuance, the management agreed, but the audience demanded its restoration. Until 1828, according to a contemporary historian of the theatre, every performance of *Macbeth* in Bath was dominated by this dance, which drew more applause 'not merely from the gallery, but from other parts of the house' than the finest scenes of the play.

Enthusiasm for plays, at least for 'good, hardened professional acting', is a characteristic Jane Austen bestows on many of her most admirable characters, as well as on the most impulsive, warm-hearted ones. Charles Musgrove knows his mother loves a play, Captain Wentworth readily accepts a seat in his box, and Anne would greatly prefer it to yet another formal private party of the type she detests. Catherine Morland, as we have seen, cannot resist a play, and though at one point she fears that a love of the theatre is not among the many perfections of the Tilney family, she is happily proved wrong. The case is otherwise with that other regular Bath entertainment, the concert. As far as is known, Catherine attends only one, and has not a word to say about it. Jane Austen herself is even worse (from a music-lover's point of view) since, as has been pointed out, when writing about one of Rauzzini's concerts she sounds very much like her own Isabella Thorpe.[18]

The concert in question was held on 17 April 1805. Martha's mother had recently died, and Cassandra was staying with Martha in the country. Jane wrote to her, 'You were very right in supposing I wore my crape sleeves to the concert, I had them put in on the occasion; on my head I wore my crape and flowers, but I do not think it looked particularly well'. This is horribly akin to Isabella Thorpe's 'Anne Mitchell had tried to put on a turban like mine, as I wore it the week before at the concert'. The principal singer at the concert attended by Jane was Elizabeth Billington, whom she heard again a year later, for Mrs Austen's letter of April 1806, already quoted, also mentions 'Rauzzini's concert last night (when Mrs Billington sang for the last time) was very full & very hot'. 'The last time' refers to that season only, since Mrs Billington was then 38 and at the height of her powers; she died in 1818.

Vincenzo Rauzzini himself died in 1810, and his prominent place in the musical life of Bath was taken by Andrew Ashe, who had married Miss Comer. 'The sweet plaintive tones of our own little Syren, Miss Comer', had been remarked upon by the *Bath*

Chronicle in 1798. It was not one of the famous Rauzzini concerts, therefore, which Anne Elliot attended in February 1815. A whole chapter is devoted to this occasion, but it is the 'little zig-zags of emotion' (to quote *Emma*) rather than the music which interest Jane Austen. Though both hero and heroine are allowed to be musical, the affectations of others do not escape censure, and 'the gapes' which Jane Austen notices with amusement were surely not unknown to herself. This is the only public entertainment that Anne is enabled to attend. Her opportunities for meeting and improving acquaintances on neutral ground, so invaluable to Catherine Morland, are sadly limited by her family's snobbery; it is most frustrating for her to be living in the same city as the man she loves, yet rarely to be sure of seeing him:

> The theatre or the rooms, where he was most likely to be, were not fashionable enough for the Elliots, whose evening amusements were solely in the elegant stupidity of private parties, in which they were getting more and more engaged; and Anne . . . was quite impatient for the concert evening. It was a concert for the benefit of a person patronised by Lady Dalrymple. Of course they must attend. It was really expected to be a good one, and Captain Wentworth was very fond of music.

Jane Austen's apparent personal hostility to music emerges again in a letter from the Queen Square lodgings written at the end of May 1799. 'There is to be a grand gala on Tuesday evening in Sydney Gardens; a concert, with Illuminations and fireworks; – to the latter Eliz: and I look forward with pleasure, & even the Concert will have more than its usual charm with me, as the gardens are large enough for me to get pretty well beyond the reach of its sound.' The advertisement of this event, published in the *Bath Chronicle* on 30 May, gives more details.

> Sydney-Garden Vauxhall – the most spacious and beautiful publick garden in the kingdom. On Tuesday next the fourth of June, there will be a Grand Gala in honour of His Majesty's Birthday, in a stile of magnificence never exceeded. The Evening's Entertainment will consist of a Concert of Vocal and Instrumental Music, in the new orchestra; in the course of which, Mr Nimroide will give his wonderful imitation of birds. Between the 2nd and 3rd acts of the concert there will be a most capital display of fireworks by Signor Invetto, who will exert the utmost of his ingenious stile to produce new and astounding effects. The illuminations will be most

brilliant, several devices and decorations being prepared.

Supper parties well accommodated; many Rooms will be open for that purpose, and sufficient attendants engaged. Every kind of refreshment will be charged as reasonable as possible. Doors to be open at five, and the concert to begin at seven o'clock. Admission 2s each.

The programme of music was detailed, consisting of three symphonies, a large number of vocals, and *God Save the King* in full chorus. In the event poor weather spoilt the gala, and, due to 'the disappointment experienced by a great number of ladies and gentlemen', as a new advertisement stated, it was repeated on 18 June. Jane's distaste for the musical part of the evening was perhaps shared by her companions, as they contrived to miss it. She wrote: 'Last night we were in Sydney Gardens again, as there was a repetition of the gala which went off so ill on the 4th. We did not go until nine, and then were in very good time for the Fireworks, which were really beautiful, & surpassing my expectations; – the illuminations too were very pretty. The weather was as favourable, as it was otherwise a fortnight ago'.

Two years later the King's birthday was celebrated in the same style. Jane was in Bath, and Cassandra expected to arrive there on Monday 1 June. On 27 May Jane wrote to her: 'I have made an engagement for you for Thursday the 4th of June; if my mother & aunt should not go to the fireworks, which I dare say they will not, I have promised to join Mr Evelyn and Miss Wood'.

Sydney Gardens played quite an important part in Jane Austen's Bath life, though she does not mention them in either of the Bath novels. In her first letter to Cassandra from Bath in 1799 she wrote: 'There was a very long list of arrivals here in the newspaper yesterday, so that we need not immediately dread absolute solitude; and there is a public breakfast in Sydney Gardens every morning, so that we shall not be wholly starved.' (It is doubtful whether she would have enjoyed the breakfasts, since they were advertised as 'attended with Horns, Clarionets, etc'.) When a house in that locality was first mooted, she wrote: 'To be near Sydney Gardens would be a pleasant circumstance; we might go into the labyrinth every day'. In the event, they found a house as close to Sydney Gardens as could possibly be, and it is to be hoped that the advantage of greenery outside their windows cancelled out any disadvantage from the noise.

Sydney Gardens contributed greatly to the summer amenities of the city, and perhaps could only have been thought of when sufficient residents were staying in Bath all the year round. Until

Sydney Gardens

the end of the century, the old bowling green, Terrace Walk on the city side of the river, and Spring Gardens on the other side, accessible only by ferry, had been deemed sufficient for outdoor recreation. But a new spirit of *rus in urbe* was abroad. The 1800 Bath Guide says:

> Sydney-Garden Vauxhall is situated at the termination of Great Pulteney street. It was opened for publick entertainment on the 11th of May 1795. This pleasure-garden was designed by Mr Harcourt Masters, Architect, in which he has displayed much taste and judgement. The stile is quite new, and exhibits the most pleasing variety. There is also an elegant and spacious Hotel. It is let to Mr Holloway, who conducts it with great spirit and liberality. The terms of subscription are 2s 6d for a month, 5s for a quarter, and 7s 6d for a season. Non-subscribers for walking 6d each, and tea is rendered at 6d. There are swings, bowling greens and a Merlin's swing in the labyrinth; a plan of which is sold at the bar at 6d each.
>
> During the summer are publick nights, with musick, fireworks and superb illuminations. Surrounding the Garden is a Ride for the accommodation of Ladies and Gentlemen on horseback, supported by a subscription of 2s 6d for one month, 5s for three months, or 15s per year; non-subscribers pay 6d each time. It commands beautiful and romantic views, and has the advantage of being free from dust in summer and dirt in winter.

Another location for sedate horseback riding was the Riding School, which Jane Austen visited twice, in December 1797 and April 1805, not in order to ride herself, but to watch the prowess of young friends. 'This morning', she wrote on the latter occasion, 'we have been to see Miss Chamberlayne look hot on horseback. – Seven years & four months ago we went to the same Riding house to see Miss Lefroy's performance! What a different set we are now moving in! But seven years I suppose are enough to change every pore of one's skin, & every feeling of one's mind.' This is the second reference which establishes the visit of November-December 1797 beyond doubt.

The Guide informs us: 'At a little distance from the New Assembly-Rooms, in Montpelier Row, is a large and commodious Riding-School, kept by Mr Dash, where Ladies and Gentlemen amuse themselves every morning, and are instructed in the art of horsemanship. The terms for those who learn to ride, and ride the managed horse, are three guineas per month (16 lessons) or

5s 3d each lesson.' By 1800 there was a second riding school, Ryles in Monmouth Street.

Every amusement cost money, and Jane, with a very limited allowance, must have had to choose carefully between them. Nowhere is this more apparent than in a remark *à propos* her stingy aunt. In April 1805 she told Cassandra:

> My Aunt is in a great hurry to pay me for my Cap, but cannot find it in her heart to give me good money. If I have any intention of going to the Grand Sydney-Garden breakfast, if there is any party I wish to join, Perrot will take out a ticket for me. Such an offer I shall of course decline; & all the service she will render me therefore, is to put it out of my power to go at all, whatever may occur to make it desirable.'

No such distresses beset Catherine Morland, who is given £10 by her father when she sets off for Bath, and promised more when she needs it. Catherine, in Bath for only a few weeks, is able to take full advantage of all the entertainments laid on. Anne Elliot is not so lucky, being forced to endure private parties that have no appeal for her. 'I am no card player', she says. Jane Austen, too, fretted to be subjected to this time-wasting habit, usually at her aunt's house. 'We are to have a tiny party here tonight; I hate tiny parties – they force one to constant exertion', and 'Another stupid party last night; perhaps if larger they might be less intolerable, but here there were only just enough to make one card table, with six people to look on, & talk nonsense to each other'. On the whole, however, she had her share of liberty and enjoyment, and her tone is not usually so jaundiced. The public entertainments of Bath afforded her various kinds of amusement personally, and furnished her novels with incident and location without which they would certainly be the poorer.

PART THREE

'We left Bath . . . '

'I really believe I shall always be talking of Bath, when I am home again – I *do* like it so very much', enthuses Catherine Morland. And yet, when the time comes for her to leave, with the superior pleasures of Northanger Abbey to look forward to, she 'caught the last view of Bath without any regret'. Back at home, she does not think or talk of Bath at all, either in her unhappiness before the arrival of Henry, or her happiness afterwards. This, Jane Austen implies, is as it should be. Catherine's youthful delight in Bath is natural and healthy, but it is only one phase in her education, and as she assumes new cares and responsibilities, Bath fades into the background: a happy memory, but nothing to regret for an instant. Mrs Allen, with her continued enthusiasm, is in comparison immature: her judgement is impugned by her continual harping on the pleasures of Bath (especially since these pleasures are chiefly fashion and shopping, rather than cultural) and by her unspecific terms of praise: 'Bath is a nice place, Catherine, after all'. This is not to say that Catherine herself ever repudiates Bath, or revises her opinions of it, merely that she effortlessly gets it into proportion.

Isabella Thorpe only feigns the disgust with Bath which she believes it fashionable to express. 'Do you know I get so immoderately sick of Bath: your brother and I were agreeing this morning that, though it is vastly well to be here for a few weeks, we would not live here for millions.' Henry Tilney knows Isabella's type only too well (which is why Catherine's freshness and honesty of response are so appealing to him); as he says, 'Bath, compared with London, has little variety, and so everybody finds out every year. For six weeks, I allow Bath is pleasant enough; but beyond *that*, it is the most tiresome place in the world. You would be told so by people of all descriptions, who come regularly every winter, lengthen their six weeks into ten or twelve, and go away at last because they can afford to stay no longer.' Henry is the cool, detached observer, neither praising nor decrying Bath himself. Though a clergyman, he does not think it wrong to participate in Bath's amusements; he is no pompous killjoy, but he does imagine (or at least hope) that Catherine must spend her time 'more rationally' in the country.

The various pressures to spend one's time to no good purpose consititute Anne's chief complaint against Bath (and her creator's too). It grieves Anne that her father 'should see nothing to regret in the duties and dignity of the resident landholder; should find so much to be vain of in the littlenesses of a town.' Anne's own feelings are straightforward: 'She disliked Bath' and 'she persisted in a very determined, though very silent, disinclination for Bath'. But the Bath she is forced to inhabit is very different from Catherine Morland's. There are no balls, no walks or drives in the country, for Anne. She finds pleasure in visiting her old school friend, but her evenings are too often frittered away in tiresome, uninteresting card parties. It is her father's and sister's chosen lifestyle and values that irk; Bath is not the cause of the Elliots' vanity and selfishness, but exposes these qualities more ruthlessly than had Kellynch. There, Anne (rather like her mother before her) had tried to overlook their faults; in Bath, where they are competing for prestige with other members of the gentry, it is impossible for Anne not to be painfully aware of them. Her sister Elizabeth's attention to form, and lack of warmth of heart and generosity, find full scope in Bath. 'Old fashioned notions', she tells herself, when pondering whether to invite the Musgroves to dinner; 'country hospitality – we do not profess to give dinners – few people in Bath do – Lady Alicia never does.' Nothing could be further from the bewitching way that the Harvilles 'invite from the heart'. Mr Elliot sums up all that Anne finds distressing and pointless when he says: 'Here you are in Bath, and the object is to be established with all the credit and dignity which ought to belong to Sir Walter Elliot'. In referring to the necessity of cultivating the dreary Lady Dalrymple and her daughter, he asserts: 'They will move in the first set in Bath this winter, and as rank is rank, your being known to be related to them will have its use in fixing your family (our family let me say) in that degree of consideration which we must all wish for'.

'In London, perhaps', Mr Elliot submits, they might be no-body; 'but in Bath, Sir Walter Elliot and his family will always be worth knowing, always acceptable as acquaintance'. This underlines the poverty of Bath society, in comparison to 50 years earlier, when Bath attracted not only the nobility, but statesmen, writers, artists, musicians: many people of brilliance and achievement. *Then*, for those within the charmed circle, the city must have been a stimulating place to stay. Now, as the shrewd Mr Shepherd knows perfectly well, Bath would be 'a much safer place' than London for an impoverished baronet: 'he might be important there at comparatively little expense'. If such nonentities as Sir Walter and Lady Dalrymple are 'important', there can be few people in Bath who fulfil Anne's more stringent criteria of 'good company'.

And yet a perfectly sensible woman like Lady Russell may take pleasure in Bath. 'Lady Russell was fond of Bath.' It is the fondness perhaps of habit; an annual visit to Bath punctuates her year, and forms the 'winter pleasures' of her rather sedate lifestyle. Besides meeting up with old friends and drinking the waters, she enjoys the mental stimulation of getting 'the new publications' as soon as they appear. Lady Russell's relish for Bath seems perfectly rational, and we are not meant to despise her for it. This regular sojourn in the city keeps her mentally and socially alert. She is perfectly sincere in thinking that the stimulation and society of Bath would be good for Anne.

Other characters who unaffectedly enjoy what Bath has to offer during a brief visit, but who have no intention of making it their home, are the Crofts. Inattentive to Sir Walter's kind of snobbery, they walk about arm in arm and stop to chat whenever they come across 'a little knot of the navy': Mrs Croft quite as prominent in these conversations as her husband. 'And then we get away from them all, and shut ourselves into our lodgings, and draw in our chairs', as the Admiral tells Anne with satisfaction. Their preference for each other's society, for being 'snug' as he calls it, combined with their unceremonious pleasure in meeting old friends, is attractive to Anne and approved by their creator.

So, attitudes to Bath are a moral barometer. Sampled moderately, and in the right, unselfish spirit, Bath promotes friendship, cultural development and social maturity. Too often, however, Jane Austen's characters are drawn to Bath for the wrong reasons: not only the Elliots and the Thorpes, but characters from the four novels which are *not* set in Bath. In these books, Bath, lurking in the background as it were, really does seem an evil influence. It is in Bath that Willoughby seduces Eliza Williams and leaves her pregnant, in *Sense and Sensibility*. In *Pride and Prejudice*, Wickham, we are told, escapes periodically from an unhappy marriage to Bath (spending money which he does not possess).

The vicious Admiral Crawford, in *Mansfield Park*, is a regular visitor to Bath: 'It is my uncle's usual time' replies Henry Crawford when Tom Bertram remarks that it is rather early in the season (October) to be going to Bath. Crawford himself is slinking off to Bath from fulfilling the expectations he has deliberately raised in Maria Bertram. In *Emma* that clergyman on the make, Philip Elton, goes to Bath in a mood of pique and returns triumphant in possession of Miss Hawkins; while Augusta Elton herself, equally satisfied with the bargain, recommends the city to the outraged Emma as good husband-hunting ground. 'The advantages of Bath to the young are pretty generally understood', she says knowingly. Mrs Elton is in no doubt that 'my Bath life' has given her a polish and a knowledge of the world which Emma lacks.

Besides the snobbery and formality, the time-wasting, the frivolity and the dubious motives of too many of its visitors, Jane Austen herself personally disliked the climate of Bath, a dislike which she made Anne Elliot share. Anne 'did not think it agreed with her' and was 'dreading the possible heats of September in all the white glare of Bath'. In the summer of 1814, Jane's friend Martha Lloyd was invited to stay with her friends the Deans Dundases in Bath. Jane wrote on 23 June to Cassandra:

> Instead of Bath the Deans Dundases have taken a house in Clifton – Richmond Terrace – and she is as glad of the change as even you or I should be, or almost. She will now be able to go on from Berks and visit them without any fears from heat.

The Deans Dundases changed their plans again, however, and on 2 September Jane wrote from London where she was staying with her brother Henry to Martha at Great Pulteney Street:

> The weather can hardly have incommoded you by its heat. We have had many evenings here so cold, that I was sure there must be fires in the country. How many alterations you must perceive in Bath! and how many people and things gone by, must be recurring to you! I hope you will see Clifton.

That Jane preferred Clifton, the Georgian suburb of Bristol in an airy, elevated situation, to Bath, in its bowl between the hills, is undeniable. (Hester Thrale Piozzi, who was fond enough of Bath, termed it a 'stewpot.') It was to Clifton, though only for a few weeks, that Jane, her mother and her sister first went when they left Bath, for ever, in the summer of 1806. Their removal was sudden; a naval brother, Frank, had invited them to share a household with himself and his new bride in Southampton: the Austens would be company for Mary while he was at sea, and the sharing of expenses would benefit everybody. Before settling in Southampton, the Austens travelled north on a round of visits to relations. But the day they left their last poor Bath home, in

Trim Street, was firmly engraved on Jane's memory. 'It is two years tomorrow', she wrote on 30 June 1808, 'since we left Bath for Clifton – with what happy feelings of escape!'

In Southampton, Jane again had the pleasure of a garden – the lack of one had been a real deprivation in Bath – and in 1809, an even more congenial move was made by the Austen ladies, to a cottage on brother Edward's Chawton estate, in their own dear countryside of Hampshire. Here, before her tragically early death in 1817, Jane experienced contentment and fulfilment, enabling her to revise the three early novels and to write three more, drawing on a knowledge of human nature, and of the society of her age, which could only have been improved during the years in Bath. She had the happiness of seeing four of her works published in her lifetime. She continued to keep in touch with Bath news, through the Leigh Perrots, who remained there, and through such visitors as Martha Lloyd and Fanny Knight, who were both there in 1814, the year in which *Persuasion* is set.

As Catherine Morland says: 'There is much more sameness in a country life than in a Bath life'. Jane Austen had the advantages of sampling both and, in the calm of her country life, she created her exquisite works of art from the materials she had mentally gathered in Bath.

Trim Bridge

Notes

1. R. S. Neale, *Bath 1680-1850: A Social History, or, A Valley of Pleasure Yet a Sink of Iniquity*, Routledge & Kegan Paul, 1981. A massive and scholarly study of the economic and social underpinnings of Bath to which I am indebted for many insights.

2. Walter Ison (see note 8) thinks that Wood was probably introduced to Chandos by another nobleman with an Austenesque name, Lord Bingley, for whom Wood had worked in Yorkshire – where, according to his own account, Wood had already begun to form plans for Bath, but without having any financial backing in view.

3. This guide book, which I have quoted from extensively, is available for consultation in Bath Reference Library, as are the contemporary issues (on microfilm) of the *Bath Chronicle* and *Bath Journal*, which I have also cited in the text.

4. All quotations from Jane Austen's letters are taken from R. W. Chapman (editor), *Jane Austen's Letters to her Sister Cassandra and Others*, O.U.P., 1979 (second edition) and are made by kind permission of the Oxford University Press.

5. Quoted from R. A. Austen-Leigh (editor), *Austen Papers 1704-1856*, Spottiswoode, Ballantyne & Co. Ltd, 1942.

6. For a full account of her travels, which extended through fourteen counties, see my *Jane Austen's England*, Robert Hale, 1986.

7. For details of all such family matters see my *Jane Austen's Family*, Robert Hale, 1984.

8,9. Walter Ison, *The Georgian Buildings of Bath*, Faber and Faber, 1948, reprinted Kingsmead Press 1969; by far the most authoritative study of the subject.

10. W. & R. A. Austen-Leigh, *Jane Austen, Her Life and Letters: A Family Record*, Smith, Elder & Co., 1913, and much quoted since.

11. I am indebted to Margaret Wilson, who is writing a biography of Fanny Knight, for most generously providing these quotations from Fanny's letters and diaries.

12. See Penelope Byrd, *A Frivolous Distinction: Fashion and Needlework in the Works of Jane Austen*, Bath City Council, 1979.

13. Maurice Berrill, 'Jane Austen and Canals', *The Jane Austen Society Report for 1960*. I am grateful to David Gilson for drawing this article to my attention.

14. Quoted in Neale (see note 1).

15. *The Wonders of a Week at Bath in doggerel address to the Hon T. G. from F. T. Esq.*

16. William Lowndes, *The Theatre Royal at Bath*, Redcliffe Press, 1982.

17. I am indebted to the researches and recent address of Margaret Kirkham to the Bath and Bristol Branch of the Jane Austen Society for making available this information.

18. Patrick Piggott, *The Innocent Diversion, Music in the Life and Writings of Jane Austen*, Cleverdon, 1979. I am also grateful to Jon Gillaspie for discussing with me the musical life of Bath in Jane Austen's time.

Map A

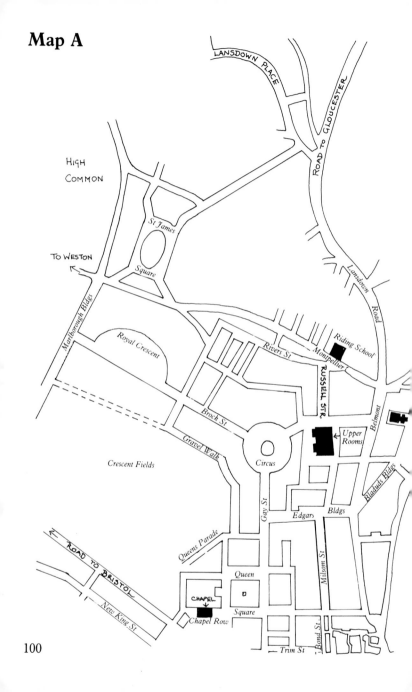

LANSDOWN PLACE

ROAD TO GLOUCESTER

HIGH COMMON

St James Square

TO WESTON

Marlborough Bldgs

Lansdown Road

Royal Crescent

Rivers St

Riding School

Montpellier

RUSSELL STR.

Brock St

Gravel Walk

Belmont

Upper Rooms

Crescent Fields

Circus

Bladuds Bldgs

Gay St

Edgars

Bldgs

Milsom St

Queens Parade

ROAD TO BRISTOL

New King St

CHAPEL

Chapel Row

Queen Square

Bond St

Trim St

100

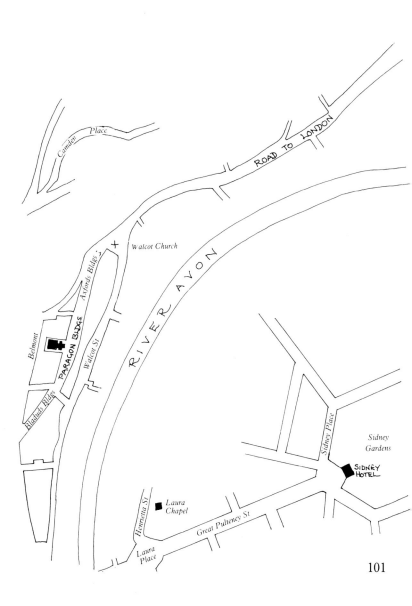

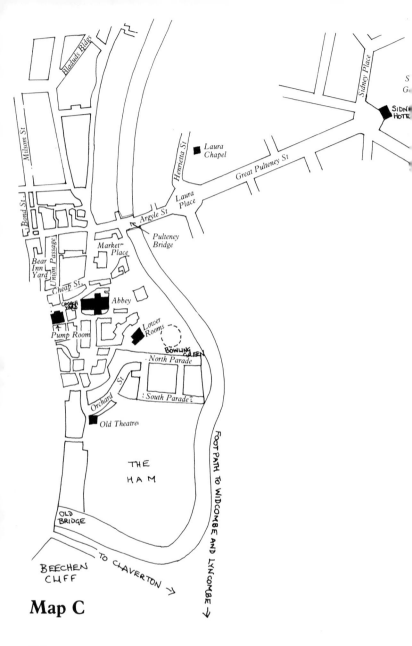

Map C

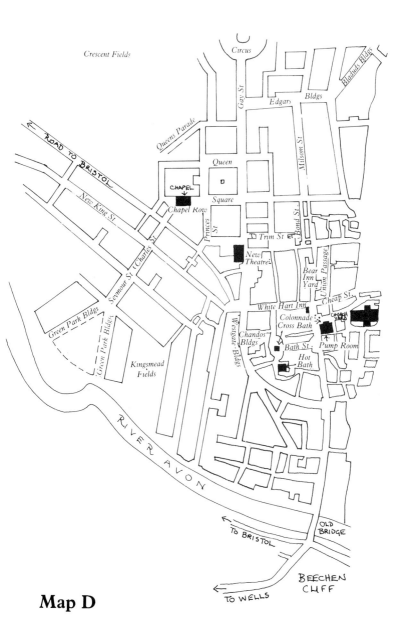

Map D

103

Index

A list of principal streets and places as at the time of Jane Austen. Figures in italic denote an illustration; the letters refer to the maps on pages 100-103.